DOHA AND QATAR

TRAVEL GUIDE

ARABESQUE TRAVEL

ISBN 978-1-9998135-9-8

Spellings are in British English. While care has been taken in the compilation of this guide things change, timings alter, places close and errors creep in. As such the publisher does not accept responsibility for loss, injury or difficulty from the use of this guide and its information.

The publisher thanks Alan Fitz-Patrick and Ibrahim Al Busafi for their assistance in creating this book. The front cover image is courtesy Konevi.

CONTENTS

CHAPTER ONE

BASIC FACTS

G eography: The State of Qatar is a peninsula situated halfway down the east coast of the Arabian Peninsula (the western coast of The Gulf), bordered to the south by Saudi Arabia.

The coastline is about 550 km long and bounds the county to the west, north and east. Low hills in the north-west and dunes in the south-east are the most distinct geography. There are several small islands including Halul, Shirawah and Al Ashat. The total land area of Qatar is approximately 11,627sq km.

Capital: Doha is the capital, economic and population centre of Qatar; see towns chapter 11.

Economy: Qatar is one of the world's wealthiest nations in terms of GDP per capita. Oil and gas is the basis of this wealth, a situation that is projected to continue for the next century.

Population: Mid-year population in 2019 is esti-mated at 2,740,000 appx giving a population density rate of

237 persons per sq km; most of which are located on Qatar's east coast. This is slightly less than the United Kingdom's 274 per sq km and far more than the very low density of the United States of America of 34 per sq km.

Climate: Qatar has a hot, humid desert climate with long summers and from November to February short warm winters.

Language: Arabic is the official language; however, English, Hindi/Urdu & Bengali are widely spoken.

Religion: Islam is the official religion of the country.

Qatar National Day: Qatar's National Day is the 18th of December & is an official holiday.

Flag: The flag is white and 'Qatar maroon" having a serrated vertical border of nine white triangles between the two colours. The colour maroon represents the imperial purple of ancient civilizations, which used dye obtained from shellfish that were exploited in Qatar.

Currency: The official currency is the Qatari Riyal (QAR), which is divided into 100 Dirhams. The exchange parity has been at a fixed rate of US$ = 3.65 QARs.

Work Hours: Government: From 07:00-14:00. Friday and Saturday are weekend holidays. Companies: typically from 08:00-12:00 / 16:00-20:00 (or 08:00 – 17:00). Friday & Saturday is the weekend.

Local Time: Three hours + Greenwich Mean Time

CHAPTER TWO

GEOGRAPHY

O n the eastern coast of the Arabian peninsula, Qatar, a peninsula itself, is one of the world's smallest countries at 11,627 sq km extending about 190km south to north and a maximum 90kilometrs east-west.

This size includes offshore islands; such as Halul, some 97km to the northeast of Doha, Al Ashat 60km south of Doha and Fasht Ad Dibal north-west of Al Ruwais. Though Qatar is smaller than the USA state of Connecticut or the British counties of Perth or Yorkshire, the size belies the extraordinary wealth of the country.

Doha looking towards West Bay

Qatar shares a single land border of 87km with Saudi Arabia and has sea borders with Bahrain to the west, the United Arab Emirates to the east and Iran to the north, in addition to the sea borders with Saudi Arabia to the south-west and southeast. In 2001 the border with Saudi Arabia was ratified, and the sea border with Bahrain was also agreed the same year. That ratification resulted in the Hawar Islands, a few hundred metres off Qatar's west coast, being confirmed as Bahraini territory. Areas disputed with Bahrain and awarded to Qatar at the same time were Al Zubarah in Qatar's north-west mainland, the scattered islets of Fasht Ad Dibal north-west of Al Zubarah and Jinan Island north-west of Dukhan. The seas near the Hawar Islands (Bahrain) and Khor Al Udaid (also called the 'Inland Sea'), part of which is in Saudi Arabia's territory, are areas where small distances of water separate different states. With the political situation between Qatar and its neighbours being especially fractious, it is essential to ensure you do not enter the water, or land, within the jurisdiction of another state.

Qatar is part of the Arabian Shelf, the eastern sedimentary areas of the Arabian Plate that is moving north and being subducted under the Iranian/Eurasian plates. The geology of Qatar includes surface areas of gravels and sandstone of the Hofuf Formation formed by rivers over the last 1.5million years. The Hofuf Formation lies over the Dam Formation of the Miocene Period (23-5million years ago approximately) which has clays and limestones and is largely found in the south-west of the country. Below the Dam formation is the Dammam Formation, much of which is a chalky limestone and dolomite. The Dammam Formation extends over most of Qatar and was created during the Middle Eocene (48-38million years ago). The Dammam Formation is a karst limestone environment that contains sinkholes and caves. Typical examples can be found off the Salwa Road to the north-west and south-east of the Rawdat Rashid Interchange GPS 25.172620, 51.327474. The sinkholes and caves are thought to have developed from about 560,000years ago. Below the Dammam Formation is the Rus Formation a chalky limestone and marl/clay formed during the Early Lower Eocene (48-38 million years ago).

The key structural elements within the Qatar rock formations are anticlines; these are rock strata that have been forced into a convex arch. It is here that the wealth of Qatar, its oil and gas, is trapped in the upper part of the arch where suitable 'capping' rock is found. The major anticlines are the Qatar Arch that extends from the south of the country into Iran; in this arch's north-east is the vast North Gas Field. Others include the Dukhan Anticline that flows

from the south to the north-west a few kilometres inland
from the coast up to the area of Dukhan. This uplift has
exposed the fossiliferous Dam Formation and has trapped
the Dukhan oilfield to its west.

Yardangs at Zekreet

Almost devoid of notable contours, Qatar's highest
point is in the south-west at Qurayn Abu al Bawl
GPS24.717757, 51.047408 (also called Al Galail), next to
a security installation so do take care regarding photography and activities here and at all government buildings in
Qatar. The location overlooks the Saudi Arabian border 19
km away taking advantage of the 103 metres elevation
access is west from the 'Qatar/UAE Rd' (route 59) at
GPS24.713951, 51.069953. The land gradually drops in
general elevation from there towards the north, though
there is a series of low hills in the north and the general flat-
ness makes any rock outcrop noteworthy. Shallow dry
valleys that are locally called *wadi* are found throughout
the country.

North of Khor Al Udaid (a *khor* is a natural inlet from
the sea) on the south-east coast are dunes and *sabkha* (mud,
sand, gypsum salt flats). The sands are aeolian (wind-blown)
in origin while the *sabkha* that often looks a solid surface

might be a quicksand-like trap waiting for unwary drivers. Khor Al Udaid is a sea inlet that forms part of Qatar's south-eastern border with Saudi Arabia. Many of the areas here are named 'pure' (نقيان) with a noun to identify the location. Perhaps the paleness of the sand gave rise to the description.

To Doha's west and north-west are areas of karst limestone with numerous depressions symptomatic of erosion and sinkholes. North of Doha the coast is sand, created following changes in the level of The Gulf which, when lower over 10,000 years ago, allowed sand from the extensive exposed seabed to be blown inland.

CHAPTER THREE

CLIMATE

Q atar's climate is a humid desert climate with scorching, humid summers, and warm winters.

Qatar's hottest month July, reaches 48Celsius (C) in Doha , with a night-time minimum of 29C, and humidity up to 90%. In January, the highest temperature might be 31C and minimum 12C with humidity up to 100% if a night fog forms, typically during the day it's around 40%. Rain is unlikely at any time of year with the highest probability during December-March. Winds are usually very light coming from the south in the summer and from the north in winter when weather systems drop south from Asia. Springtime can have dust-storms for a few days, which may originate over Iran. Note that the average is an average of both night and day.

Month average max C.

Jan - Feb - *Mar* - Apr May - Jun

23 - 25 - 30 - 35 - 41 - 43

Jul - Aug - Sep - Oct - Nov - Dec

44 - 43 - 40 - 37 - 31 - 26

CHAPTER FOUR

NATURE

With Qatar's extreme desert climate, plants and animals have constant stress to survive. Add in an increasingly developed human environment and this pressure increases.

Qatar's fauna ultimately depends on its 300+ species of flora.

Plants & Trees

The dominant trees are '*ghaf*' *Prosopis cineraria*, this large tree with its feathery leaves grows in sandy soils (though not usually in dunes) and in Qatar from the central region through to the north. The *ghaf's* leaves can trap fog and the resultant water dripping to the ground becomes the tree's own irrigation system. The Christ's thorn tree *Ziziphus spina-christi* grows in rocky *wadi* environments; the flowers are a source of prized honey, and its small fruit is eaten by animals and, in the recent past, by humans. Its densely branched habit and 20 metres height make it an ideal as a shade tree, so it was planted in villages. A similar tree *Ziziphus mauritiana* has been introduced, probably from Malaysia.

Acacia tortils

Three species of Acacia are found, '*Salam*' - *Acacia ehrenbergiana* is found in open sandy soils. Its appearance varies but is usually a very ragged bushy shape of less than three metres. '*Garat*' - *Acacia nilotica* has a similar appearance to Salam, though slightly smaller and less bushy. '*Simr*' *Acacia tortilis* / *Vachellia tortilis* is spread throughout Qatar and, as with other Acacias, prefers well-drained sandy soil. This tree is the classic umbrella Acacia found in Africa, and unlike the other Acacia of Qatar, its flower is creamy coloured rather than yellow. All Acacia have roots that can penetrate deep into the soil and rock, perhaps up to 30metres depth, in search of water. The trees respond to drought by dropping their leaves, which will regrow rapidly after rains.

On the north coasts and at Al Wakrah, south of Doha, Mangrove *Avicennia marina* grows on muddy areas in the intertidal zone. In Qatar, around Al Thakira, they grow up to around five metres. Mangrove's aerial roots allow absorption of oxygen, water and nutrients in a muddy stagnate lagoon type environment, while the leaves excrete salts from seawater.

Mammals

Qatar's land mammals in historical times may have included the Asiatic lion and Asiatic cheetah along with their prey that would have included antelope and gazelle. Today the numbers of land mammals and their variety has reduced. Smaller mammals are the most common.

Dwarf gerbil *Gerbillus nanus* Wagner's gerbil *Gerbillus dasyurus* Cheesman's gerbil *Gerbillus cheesmani*are are widely dispersed small rodents. Cheesman's gerbil is probably the most readily seen towards dusk in sandy areas. Look for a light russet colour rodent about 11 centimetres (cm) in body length with a slightly longer tail, and rear legs that are somewhat longer than the forelegs. These are opportunistic feeders, preferring seeds & grain though eating insects if other food is scarce. They probably breed throughout the year, and each litter may have up to eight young. They are vital food for owls and foxes. Jirds are related to gerbils, though they are larger at up to 16cm with a more rat-like appearance. The Libyan jird *Meriones libycus* and Sundevall's jird *Meriones crassus* are omnivorous and occupy sandy or rocky desert in Qatar. With its long kangaroo type rear legs, the Egyptian jerboa *Jaculus jaculus* occupy a similar niche to the gerbil. The more familiar house mouse *Mus musculus* and house rat *Rattus rattus* join these small rodents in Qatar.

The desert hedgehog *Paraechinus aethiopicus* at up to 25 cm is a relatively small hedgehog. As with most other hedgehogs, this is a nocturnal animal that eats insects and small animals. With a litter of perhaps six young, this hedgehog breeds once a year. Cape hare *Lepus capensis* is comparable to the European brown hare in appearance and is up to 68cm in length. As with most other desert animals, this is active from dusk to dawn, sheltering under vegetation during the day. This animal breeds throughout the year with perhaps six litters annually and four leverets in each. Its adult size and the lack of larger predators mean that it is most vulnerable only when young.

The largest predators in Qatar include three canids and possibly the honey badger *Mellivora capensis* which might live in the south of the country. The honey badger is omnivorous, about 75cm long excluding the tail and may have a couple of cubs.

Golden jackal *Canis aureus* is an adaptive predator with a body length up to 85cm long and a tail of about 25cm with a weight of 14kilograms (kg) with a coat of a rusty brown with black back. It is possible that this jackal breeds with feral dogs in Qatar. It is both a hunter of small rodents and lizards as well as scavenging including fruit and vegetation. They breed once a year and give birth to up to six pups. The red fox *Vulpes vulpes arabica* is found throughout Qatar and is a subspecies of the red fox, with a less intense red colour. Ruppell's fox *Vulpes rueppelli sabaea* is a pale coloured desert-living fox up to 74cm long including its tail, and the animal weighs less than 1.9kg. They breed once a year with up to six pups. This fox, as with many others, is omnivorous eating small animals, large insects and vegetation.

Bats include desert long-eared bat *Otonycteris hemprichii* and Geoffrey's trident leaf-nosed bat *Asellia tridens* which are both insectivorous.

Arabian oryx

Reintroduced species include the **Arabian oryx** *Oryx leucoryx* which has become the logo of Qatar Airways. The oryx can be up to 175cm long, 100cm at shoulder height and weigh up to 100kg with both sexes having twin horns of up to 65cm. Their natural habitat is a desert environment, both stony and sandy, where they might roam in large family groups of about ten animals. The white colour of the coat helps reflect the heat, while in colder weather the hair raises to expose the darker skin allowing it to absorb heat.

The Arabian oryx can breed throughout the year with a single calf born after eight months of mating. The calf is well camouflaged with a mid brown coat. Extinct in the wild throughout the world by 1972 due to hunting, a breeding population had been established in several zoos, most importantly at Phoenix and San Diego Zoos around the world and animals were reintroduced into their original countries from the mid-1970s. In Qatar this reintroduction was focused initially on Al Wabra Wildlife Preservation, a private zoo; later other locations bred the animal. The Arabian oryx is a herbivore which in winter can obtain its water from fresh vegetation that includes grasses and leaves.

The other major mammal reintroduced to Qatar is the Arabian sand gazelle *Gazella subgutturosa marica*. Due to hunting, the animal was extinct in Qatar by the end of the 1950s and was reintroduced in the mid-1990s, notably in Al Reem Reserve. The males can grow to a length of 120cm and weigh 30kg. Both sexes have horns, though the male's are substantially larger.

Arabian sand gazelle

In a safe environment their population growth can be rapid as this gazelle can breed after it is about 18months old, and in about 30% of live births twins are born after a gestation period of just over five months.

CAMEL

Qatar would hardly seem an Arab country without the camel *Camelus dromedaries*, the dromedary (the use of camel, except where noted below refers to *Camelus dromedaries*).

The world camel comes from the Arabic جمل (*jamal*, a male camel) and the word dromedary, the single-humped variety, from the Greek *dromus*, meaning race/race course or running, all very apt in the world of Camel racing today. All living dromedaries are domesticated animals, the wild type having disappeared perhaps 2,500 years ago. This domestication happened at least by 1,000BC, probably in south-east Arabia during the period of a substantial reduction in the wild camel population.

Male camels can be two meters in height at the shoulder and weigh 600kg, females are perhaps 10% smaller in height and 30% less in weight. The single hump is a fat bearing organ and as fat can release water, if used due to lack of food, it allows better survival in drought. The diet for the camel is plants, both by grazing on the ground and browsing bushes and trees, though nowadays a large proportion is supplied as hay or other animal feed. As with a cow, the camel is a ruminant; therefore much of the day is normally spent either eating or ruminating! To cope with the desert climate, the body temperature can fluctuate by more than 10C and can deal with a 30% water loss; either of these changes would kill most mammals.

Camels Souq Waqif

Camels, fortunately, can replenish water at around 20 litres a minute, useful when in a desert climate.

From around four years, the camel can breed, with typically a single baby born after a gestation period of some 15 months. The animal may then live for some 50 years. In captivity, the dromedary has bred with the llama. In the wild, in areas such as Iran where their ranges overlap, dromedaries can breed with the two-humped Bactrian camel. In Turkey, the breeding of Bactrian and dromedary is specifically done at Izmir Province where the result is large single-humped animals, whose males compete in camel 'wrestling' events. Camels have been used historically for transport, milk, meat, clothing and more; it is probably as potentially useful as cattle, if not more.

Today in Qatar, they are bred for the prestige they bring, especially for racing. Camels are used for short races from about aged 18 months – 24months, the prime age is around six years, and older camels can race at around 40kmph. Though children were used as jockeys for their light-weight, from 2007 the 'rider' has been a simple robot, with a rotating whip to encourage the animal's speed. Prizes are up to hundreds of thousands of Qatari Riyals and luxury cars, however the most sought after rewards are the prestige of owning a winning animal though the sales value of the winner, which can reach USD 1,500,000, is an added benefit. These prices are obtained for animals which, like thoroughbred racehorses, have a known and admired lineage. Other admired camels might take part in camel beauty contests, or milking contests and again the value of an animal might run too much more than USD1,000,000 with the most expensive ever being sold for USD 2,720,000. As they say, beauty is in the eye of the beholder.

BIRDS

Currently, there have been 325 birds recorded in Qatar, excluding introductions such as the red-necked ostrich which is effectively a zoo-based bird in Qatar. Of these about 119 are relatively common, 83 are scarce but expected to be seen at some stage in the year, 38 are seen regularly but are uncommon, some 39 have only been seen one or two times, and there are around 46 vagrants. The overall number of species seen in Qatar is gradually increasing, principally as a result of new environments being created by man. These critical environments include vegetated areas such as farms, parks and golf clubs.

Three invasive species are probably amongst the most easily birds seen around Doha. The Indian mynah *Acridotheres tristis* is an aggressive resident breeding throughout Doha and surrounds. It out-competes and can kill young of similar sized birds and lives very freely along-

side people. The Indian house crow *Corvus splendens* nests
in trees and is found towards the coast in areas of human
habitation. The house crow scavenges refuse and, like the
mynah, can live alongside people. From Africa or India the
rose-ringed parakeet *Psittacula krameri* is a common resident breeder and like the mynah probably results from
escaped cage birds. This is the parakeet seen in London and
other cities worldwide that were not part of its original
range. This bird feeds on nuts, fruit and seeds and therefore
can damage cultivation in Qatar.

Off the coast of Doha at Al Aaliya Island (a restricted
location north of The Pearl) some 500 pairs of Socotra
cormorant *Phalacrocorax nigrogularis* nest. This endan-
gered species breed in winter in various months, but always
as a synchronised event in any given colony. The great
cormorant Phalacrocorax *carbo* also occurs, though in lower
numbers.

Socotra cormorant

Readily seen coast birds include greater flamingo
Phoenicopterus roseus from around November to April.
They might also be found inland at Irkhaya Farm

GPS25.013227, 51.163256 along with the black-crowned night Heron *Nycticorax nycticorax*; grey heron *Ardea cinerea*; purple heron Ardea *purpurea*. Smaller shorebirds are mostly winter visitors and include grey plover *Pluvialis squatarola*; common ringed plover *Charadrius hiaticula* ; little ringed plover *Charadrius dubius*; Kentish plover *Charadrius alexandrines*; lesser sand plover *Charadrius atrifrons*; greater sand plover *Charadrius leschenaultia*; common snipe *Gallinago gallinago*; European black-tailed godwit *Limosa limosa*; bar-tailed godwit *Limosa lapponica*; Eurasian whimbrel *Numenius phaeopus*; Eurasian curlew *Numenius arquata*; common redshank *Tringa tetanus*; marsh sandpiper *Tringa stagnatilis*; common greenshank *Tringa nebularia*; green sandpiper *Tringa ochropus*; wood sandpiper *Tringa glareola*; Terek sandpiper *Xenus cinereus*; common sandpiper *Actitis hypoleucos*; ruddy turnstone *Arenaria interpres*; sanderling *Calidris alba*; little stint *Calidris minuta*; dunlin *Calidris alpine*.

Gulls and terns which are mostly migratory species include slender-billed gull *Chroicocephalus genei*; common black-headed gull *Chroicocephalus ridibundus*; great black-headed gull *Larus ichthyaetus*; steppe gull *Larus barabensis*; gull-billed tern *Gelochelidon nilotica*; Caspian tern *Hydroprogne caspia*; lesser crested tern *Thalasseus bengalensis*; white-winged tern *Chlidonias leucopterus*; Saunders's tern *Sternula saundersi* (seen throughout the year); whiskered tern *Chlidonias hybrid* (seen throughout the year).

European roller

Inland from Doha, some attractive migrants that should be seen include the flashing blue of the European roller *Coracias garrulous*; blue-cheeked bee-eater *Merops persicus*; European bee-eater *Merops apiaster*;Eurasian hoopoe *Upupa epops* which though most migrate through Qatar some stay rather than moving on.

Expect to see common kestrel *Falco tinnunculus* and Western osprey *Pandion haliaetus* which is resident along much of the coast and breeds in Qatar. Arriving in winter are Western marsh harrier *Circus aeruginosus* and Pallid Harrier *Circus haliaetus*.

Smaller migratory species include the much sought after hypocolius *Hypocolius ampelinus* found in scrub, rufous-tailed scrub robin *Erythropygia galactotes*; spotted flycatcher *Muscicapa striata*; red-spotted bluethroat *Luscinia svecica*; black redstart *Phoenicurus ochruros*; common redstart *Phoenicurus phoenicurus*; rufous-tailed rock thrush *Monticola saxatilis*; whinchat *Saxicola rubetra*; European stonechat *Saxicola rubicola*; Northern wheatear *Oenanthe oenanthe*; Isabelline wheatear *Oenanthe isabel-*

lina; desert wheatear *Oenanthe deserti*; pied wheatear *Oenanthe pleschanka*.

Less common birds include crab-plover *Dromas ardeola* at Simaisma 30km north of Doha, though the resort there may impact their numbers. North African red-necked ostrich *Struthio camelus camelus* has been introduced to the Al Reem reserve.

Lizards

Geckos are the most numerous lizard, in species and overall numbers; Arabian desert gecko *Bunopus tuberculatus*; rough-tailed gecko *Cyrtopodion scabrum*; Heyden's gecko *Hemidactylus robustus* are all found.

The yellow-belly house gecko *Hemidactylus flaviviridis* that as its name suggests is the species commonly seen inside buildings where they feed on insects, is most probably the most commonly seen lizard in Qatar.

Other lizards include Persian leaf-toed gecko *Hemidactylus persicus*; Arabian short-fingered gecko *Stenodactylus arabicus*; Slevin's short-fingered gecko *Stenodactylus slevini*; Doria's comb-fingered gecko *Stenodactylus doriae*; Gulf short-fingered gecko *Pseudoceramodactylus khobarensis*; Iranian rock gecko *Pristurus rupestris*; Schmidt's fringe-toed lizard *Acanthodactylus schmidti*; Arabian desert lizard *Acanthodactylus opheodurus*; Blanford's short-nosed desert lizard *Mesalina brevirostris*; Hadhramaut sand lizard *Mesalina adramitana*; yellow-spotted agama *Trapelus flavimaculatus*; Arabian toad-headed agama *Phrynocephalus arabicus*; Eastern skink *Scincus mitranus*; Southern grass skink *Heremites septemtaeniatus*.

Arabian toad-headed agama

The strangest lizard of Qatar is Zarudny's worm lizard *Diplometopon zarudnyi,* a limbless subterranean lizard. The largest lizards are desert monitor *Varanus griseus* which can reach over 90cm from the nose to the tip of the tail, and Egyptian spiny-tailed lizard *Uromastyx aegyptia* which is slightly smaller at up to 80cm.

There is a toad species, the African common toad *Sclerophrys regularis* that may have been introduced from Egypt.

Snakes include Sindh saw-scaled viper *Echis carinatus sochureki* a venomous ambush hunter; possibly the desert black snake *Walterinnesia aegyptia* a venomous hunter of small animals; hooded malpolon / false cobra *Malpolon moilensis* a venomous rodent eater; Hardwicke's rat snake *Coluber ventromaculatus* found in vegetation; flowerpot snake *Rhamphotyphlops braminus* a worm-like snake found in soil; crowned dwarf snake *Eirenis coronella coronella*; crowned leaf-nosed snake *Lytorhynchus diadema*; Clifford's diadem snake *Spalerosophis diadema cliffordi* a six foot long hunter of rodents.

Moths and butterflies of Qatar are throught to number less than 35 species including the Blue pansy *Junonia orithya*; Clouded yellow *Colias croceus*; Painted lady *Vanessa cardui*, whose family is also familiar in Europe.

MARINE

Despite being almost landlocked and shallow, The Gulf (this phrase is used in this book rather than the Arabian Gulf that is used in the Arab world or Persian Gulf that is used elsewhere) has many sea mammals including orca / killer whale *Orcinus orca*; Byrdes whale *Balaenoptera edeni*; Indo-Pacific bottlenose dolphin *Tursiops aduncus*; Indo-Pacific humpbacked dolphin *Sousa chinensis*; spinner dolphin *Stenella longirostris*; often seen leaping out of the sea and rotating its body and dugong *Dugong dugong*. The **dugong** can grow to around three metres and weigh some 500kg. They feed in shallow waters on seagrass, which means The Gulf is an ideal habitat. A single calf is born after a year's pregnancy and is dependent for almost two years after which it might live for a further 65 years.

Sea turtles

The Arabian Sea is home to several sea reptiles

including the hawksbill turtle *Eretmochelys imbricate* and green turtle *Chelonia mydas* both of which are found in Qatar's seas. Perversely green turtles are the most common in the waters where they feed on seagrass but do not appear to nest in Qatar, while hawksbill do nest, but the adults move elsewhere to feed in coral reefs. The hawksbill has a hawk beak -like shaped mouth, while the green turtle's is more rounded. The green turtle gets its name from the green tinge to its fat.

Green Turtle

The most detailed knowledge of any turtle is for the green turtle; however, it is likely that in most respects the hawksbill is similar.

A mature adult green turtle may measure 120cm shell length and weigh 170kg while a Hawksbill may measure 85cm and weigh 65kg. The female hawksbill may reach maturity around 20 years and green turtle from 25 onwards. Only female turtles return to the land and then only to lay eggs; males never return to land after hatching. Mating for turtles takes place at sea near the beach, following which the female will lay eggs perhaps up to 140, with the green turtle repeating this four times over a few weeks. The eggs are laid in a sandy beach, with a relatively shallow slope; in Qatar, Fuwayrit beach is a prime location. This beach is closed as a result at peak nesting season 1st April to 31 July.

As with many other reptiles, the temperature of the environment that surrounds the egg determines the sex of the hatchling, with more females developing with a temperature over 30C and more males under 30C. Global warming will affect the ratio. The nesting process is designed to camouflage the location of the eggs, but even so, foxes may locate and dig up a nest and eat the eggs. Around 60 days after the eggs are laid they hatch, and the hatchlings will co-ordinate their eruption from the nest so they emerge en-mass and scramble together towards the sea. On their way to the sea the hatchlings are predated by ghost crabs *Ocypode rotundata*, gulls, foxes and in the sea by fish. The result of this predation and other death-causes is that perhaps 995 out of every 1,000 eggs laid may never give rise to an adult. The young turtle may spend the next five years in open waters feeding on krill and other small marine life before moving to shallow waters.

After nesting the adults then leave, migrating to feeding grounds that may be hundreds of kilometres away. Each Turtle returns to breed after 2-3 years, undoubtedly returning to their hatching beach to breed when they mature.

The green turtle feeds on seagrass and algae while hawksbill are omnivorous, though preferring sea sponges, which though toxic to many sea animals do not affect the hawksbill turtle.

Other reptiles include various **sea snakes.** These are found generally in shallow waters and are best given a wide berth, annulated sea snake *Hydrophis cyanocinctus*; the gulf sea snake *Hydrophis lapemoides*; reef sea snake *Hydrophis ornatus* in shallow water including sandy bottomed areas, yellow sea snake *Hydrophis spiralis*; yellow bellied sea snake *Pelamis platurus* which this may reach over two metres and does inhabit shallow water.

CHAPTER FIVE

AGRICULTURE

Searing heat, intense sun and lack of rain mean that agriculture in Qatar depends on man-made assistance, including permanent irrigation. Farming as a result has always been subsistence with limited scope for crops and animal grazing needing a vast range.

Perhaps the key reason that man has been able to survive has been access to the sea and a symbiotic relationship with the camel. Diving for pearls has been suggested from excavations at more than a dozen sites on the coast of Eastern Arabia that date from between the 6th-4th millennium BC. This pearl diving was a seasonal practice, which in historical times was concentrated between April-September with the pearls exported, probably to Mesopotamia.

North of Doha is Al Khor's Jazirat Bin Ghanim also called Al Khor Island and 'Purple Island'. This reference to purple comes from its use in the exploitation of purple dye from a shellfish *Thais savigny* a murex sea snail. Vast quan-

tities of the shellfish produce a dye that is a variety of
"Tyrian purple" the imperial purple of Rome and elsewhere. About 45km north of Doha the island is low lying
and small at around 500metres length.

Excavations of a Bronze Age (from 2,000 BC) site have
revealed ample evidence of fish and mollusc exploitation,
tools included fishhooks. Shell middens excavated here
attest to a lengthy timeline of occupation of this site by
possibly nomadic herders/fishers along with structures that
appear to have had a cycle of use, abandonment and then
reuse, over hundreds of years, perhaps as a base for seasonal
activities such as pearling.

Historically in Qatar, the produce of domestic sheep
and goats, such as milk, meat, leather and bone were
supplemented with that from camels, which had been
domesticated by 1000BC, camels were additionally useful
in Arabia as a riding and pack animal.

There are no permanent rivers in Qatar so most water,
until recently, was as a direct result of local rain. There are
dozens of small, localised water catchment areas that can
allow small-scale subsistence crop planting. Qatar's soils are
relatively shallow, with high salt levels and low nutrients as
a result of the high evaporation and high temperatures. The
restrictions do make any form of crop cultivation difficult.

From the Bronze Age, date palms were harvested,
however until recently the lack of the volume of water
needed for successful cultivation must have made their
cultivation a peripheral activity.

Today most water for agricultural use is pumped up
from two aquifers the Aruma aquifer in south-west Qatar
(that is recharged from the west and Saudi Arabia) and the
more important Rus aquifer north-west of Doha.

Agriculture is possible over less than 300sq kilometres of Qatar, while the actual use is 83sq kilometres. The quintessential tree of Arabia the **date palm** *Phoenix dactylifera* is grown over about 24sq kilometres in Qatar. The cultivated date tree is almost entirely dependent on man for fruit production. The tree is single sex, and therefore female flowering trees need a male tree for pollination. As male trees do not produce fruit and thus 'waste' space, an artificial ratio is created of around one male tree to 100 female trees resulting in each female tree requiring artificial pollination. The tree can grow to a height of around 20 metres, and live up to approximately 90 years. All aspects of the tree and date fruit cultivation are labour intensive however the fruit, which ripens in mid-summer, can have high value and its high sugar content that preserves it, means that it can be dried and stored for perhaps two years. With all this work, Qatar now has some 500,000 trees producing about 21,000 tons of fruit.

Root vegetables grown include beet, carrots, onions and potatoes, while greenhouse crops include cucumbers, peppers, strawberries and tomatoes. Wheat imports are over 250,000tons and other fruit and vegetables are almost all imported.

Livestock animals in Qatar include more than 128,000 head of sheep, 78,000 goats, 10,000 cattle that are principally used as dairy cows. These animals are mainly imported or the descendants of recently imported animals. There are also around 24,000 camels, which are a mix of local origin and imported animals. Poultry and egg production can provide over 600,000kg of meat a year and 250,000,000 eggs. With the economic blockade of Qatar, the country hopes to improve its food security. In addition there are around 1,000 horses, a newly favoured animal, seen in equestrian centres and also in Souq Waqif.

These animals are reliant on feed being provided, and so the grass fodder is grown on large pivot fields in the south and north of the country. This fodder may be fed fresh if grown on the cattle farm, or as hay.

CHAPTER SIX

HISTORY

Q atar's history is interwoven with the surrounding regions and in many cases has to be inferred from the larger picture of the region.

On the slopes of Wadi Fatimah in central Saudi Arabia, the archaeological site at Saffaqah has remains from the Acheulean Period (1,760,000 – 130,000 years ago). Saffaqah lies in the headwaters of the major extinct river Wadi Sahba, which flowed east to towards what is now The Gulf (Arabian / Persian) immediately east of Khor Al Udaid in Qatar. This natural route allowed humans to travel very easily during an 'out of Africa' event along a fertile river valley into the region of Qatar. The earliest dated human evidence found in Qatar have been 'Abbevil-lian' stone cores (a period around 600,000-500,000 years ago) corresponding to the Lower Acheulean Period identified by Dr Julie Scott-Jackson and team of the University of Oxford. These were found in south-west Qatar (near the Saudi Arabian border) at sites collectively named 'Kapel'. The rise in sea levels over the last 15,000 years will have covered evidence of occupation by humans in the estuary of the now fossil river valley and other coastal areas.

The Gulf's size has varied with the increase and decrease of ice cover in northern and southern latitudes over the last 300,000 years. As recently as 10,000 years ago, it was a flood plain or a fertile valley for the river formed by what is now the Shatt Al Arab in Iraq. Since then, water levels have risen covering what must have been ideal living space for both animal and human populations. At times the rise in sea levels created swamps to the south of Qatar, effectively making Qatar an island.

On the west coast at Al Daasa, 6km south-east of Dukhan, pottery from the Mesopotamian civilisation of Ubaid 6500 — c. 3800 BC has been excavated scattered in a seasonal fishing settlement. Also from this period, 18 cairn burials have been found on low hills just north-west of Al Khor, north of Doha, with a pit burial covered with slabs of limestone. Later evidence of human occupation has also been found on nearby Jazirat Bin Ghanim (Purple Island), in the lagoon at Al Khor. Here remain of tools, shell and fish have been carbon dated to 5340-5080 and 5610-5285 BC. Ceramics from the Dilmun civilisation 2000-1750BC (Bronze Age) occupation with evidence of circular huts, postholes, stone-lined pits and fire hearths. Kassite pottery (from Mesopotamia 1530-1160BC) were widely distributed over this island and it is this period to which the name 'Purple Island' refers. The Kassites traded in the colour-fast dye "Tyrian purple" the imperial purple of antiquity. Evidence on this island has also been found from the Sassanid (AD 224-651) Persian occupation in the form of pottery and also pottery from AD 1700-1900. Remarkably, for 4,000 years, a small island of less than 17 hectares was considered an excellent location to work on.

At another long established site, Ras Abrouq north of Zekreet, Ubaid period (6500-3800BC) potsherds have been found. Also at Ras Abrouq are some 100 Seleucid (312-63BC) period burial cairns.

The number of these sites suggest that Qatar was a flourishing location for pre-historic man.

The first definitive reference to Qatar in historical records is by Pliny the Elder (AD 23-79) in his Natural History when he referred to a tribe the "Catharrei".

Qatar became subsumed by the rising power of the new Sassanid ruling dynasty in Persia. In AD 224 Ardashir I the Sasanian king defeated the Artabanus V, the Parthian king and founded the Persian Sassanid Empire becoming *Shahanshah* (King of Kings). He conducted military excursions around Yamama (south of modern Riyadh) in AD240, where he is reputed to have killed the ruler. He also campaigned in Mazun (modern northern Oman) which became a province of the Persian Empire under the Arab Julanda governors meaning that much of Eastern Arabia was ruled by Persia. A successor, *Shahanshah* Sapur II (AD 309-79) occupied Yamama following raid from Arabs into the Persian coast, setting up a buffer kingdom that eventually was ruled by the neighbouring Arab Lakhmid rulers, who may well have been the source of those raiding ships. Sapur II also set up frontier posts along the eastern coast of Arabia through Qatar to northern Oman and crossed west into the Hijaz and up to Syria. Following a period where little subsequent Persian activity is known, further expansion into Arabia was made during the time of *Shahanshah* Kusrow I in AD 532. This expansion by Persia included the Red Sea areas of Hijaz and Yemen, bringing Qatar from the western edge of the Persian Empire towards its geographical centre. However by AD588 Arabs were again raiding into Iran and the new *Shahanshah* Khosrow II occupied north-east Arabia and deposed the Lakhmid dynasty in AD 600. The buffer client kingdom having been removed there was easy access into Persia for the next wave of Arab invasions, the Muslim conquest.

CHRISTIANITY

Christianity was established in Qatar before the middle of the 4th century AD. The establishment of Christianity might have been a result of the relocation of monks after the persecutions carried out by *Shahanshah* Shapur II in Persia, which was probably a reaction to the Roman Emperor Constantine the Great's support of Christianity after the Edict of Milan in AD 313. A publication the 'Vitae Ionae' which is the story of a monk who lived during the time of Catholicos Barbashemin (AD 343-346), mentions a monastery of Rabban Thomas in "Beth Qatraye", modern Qatar. Beth Qatraye was one of several Christian establishments belonging to the Eastern Church in The Gulf area including on Sir Bani Yas Island (near Abu Dhabi), Bahrain, Darin Island (on the coast near Dammam Saudi Arabia) and Rew-Ardashir in Fars, northwest Persia that oversaw the others. Rew-Ardashir itself was under the administration of the bishop (later titled Catholicos) of Seleucia-Ctesiphon, the Persian capital in modern Iraq. Beth Qatraye was also the name of the ecclesiastical province that covered the current regions of Kuwait, Eastern Saudi Arabia, Bahrain and Qatar. The neighbouring ecclesiastical province of Beth Mazunaye (the Persian province of Mazun, modern Oman) was noted as attending the Markabta Synod represented by their Bishop Yohannon. In AD576 a Bishop mentions that a monastery from Beth Qatraye participated at the Synod of *Mar* Ezekiel who was the patriarch of the Eastern Church

from AD 570 -581 (*Mar* is an honorific used for Saints
and also in this case Bishops). *Mar* Ezekiel personally
visited the region and reported on the pearl fishing to
Shahanshah Khosrow I (also known as Chosroes and
Anushiruwan the Just). Beth Qatraye hermit monks
requested that Patriarch Ishoyahb I (AD582-95) of Seleucia-Ctesiphon correspond directly to them, effectively
creating their independent role in the area. In AD613 a
man, Ishaq an-Naynuwi, was born in Beth Qatraye and
was later created Bishop of Ninevah in modern Iraq and
after his death in about AD 700, he became St Isaac of
Ninevah. In AD676, well after the establishment of Islam,
the Catholicos of Seleucia-Ctesiphon held a synod at
Darin Island (off the west coast of the Arabian Peninsula
opposite Bahrain, and a Metropolitan of Beth Qatraye
attended. Beth Qatraye continued as a Christian establishment, becoming tax collectors for the Muslim rulers until
the end of the 7th Century AD. It was still recorded in the
9th Century AD and perhaps disappearing around the
time of the rise of the Qaramita state that was based in
Bahrain from AD899.

THE RISE OF ISLAM

In AD 628, Prophet Mohammed sent an envoy Abu
Al-Alaa Al-Hadrami to Munzir ibn Sawa Al Tamimi, the
governor of Qatar and the surrounding area for Persia.
Similar requests were sent to all rulers of lands abutting the
Hijaz. The letter asked for his allegiance to the Islamic faith
which Munzir ibn Sawa Al Tamimi and some of his
subjects did. After more correspondence, Mohammed
advised that those who did not become Muslims should pay
Jizya (taxation on non-Muslims). After the death of the
Prophet Mohammed in AD632, a widespread revolt
occurred throughout the Islamic world. Abu Al-Alaa Al-

Hadrami was sent again to Eastern Arabia by the new Caliph to defeat the rebels, in which he succeeded.

After the rise of the Islamic Abbasid Caliphate from AD750, the capital of the Islamic world became Baghdad in AD762. This relocation of power to the region north of Qatar created a flow of wealth through The Gulf, into what was probably the most populous city in the world who splendour was recounted in the 1001 Nights. Little, however, is known about the history of Qatar during this period.

What may be the Abbasid governor of Qatar's palace from around AD 805–885 and its supporting settlement is at Murwab in north-west Qatar, an early suggestion of the importance that this area would have.

From AD874 a new Islamic group, the Qarmatians, developed a form of Shia Islam whose core was in Bahrain. In AD899, they took advantage of a rebellion in Basra Iraq against Abbasid rule and seized power in Bahrain, Qatar and Eastern Arabia, at times stretching as far south-east as the coast of Oman. They became the most powerful force in eastern and central Arabia, exacting tribute and customs until a defeat in AD976 by the Abbasid Caliphs, after which their power was reduced. Around AD1067 the Qarmatians were overpowered, and a successor state was ruled by the Uyunid dynasty who again ruled in eastern and much of central Arabia; they owed allegiance to the Abbasids.

The occupation and destruction of Abbasid Bagdad by the Mongol prince, Hulagu Khan, in AD 1258 ushered in a period of rule of Syria, Iraq and Persia by the various Ilkhanate successors of Hulagu Khan. Qatar was on the periphery of the Ilkhanate, whose capital was in Tabriz Iran. In AD1534 Baghdad was conquered by the Ottoman

Turks and shortly after the port city of Basra also became
an Ottoman province. These various actions brought about
a long period where events in Qatar are obscure, although it
is known that from AD1253 the Bahrain based Usfurids
ruled over Eastern Arabia. They were often vassals to the
growing power of the Island Kingdom of Hormuz at the
entrance to The Gulf, itself a nominal vassal to various
Persian princes.

At the southern end of The Gulf, the Portuguese
arrived in AD1507 and defeated the rulers of the island of
Hormuz. This island kingdom dominated the southern
entrance to The Gulf and its subsequent occupation by
Portugal in AD1515 also them to establish forts in The
Gulf including three on Bahrain. The Ottomans in Basra
and Portuguese clashed frequently between AD 1550 and
AD 1560 with Portugal occupying Qatif on the Arabian
mainland opposite their fort in Bahrain and the Ottomans
occupying Al Ahsa (also called Al Hasa), in Eastern Arabia
70km inland from Qatif, on the coast opposite Bahrain. In
AD 1602 the expansion of Persia under its Safavid dynasty
ruler Shah Abbas the Great reached Bahrain, and in
AD1622, they defeated Portugal and in the same year
occupied Hormuz with the support of an English fleet.

Though Qatar was in the centre of an area of intense
competition for territory by four regional powers, it does
not seem to have been occupied, though presumably ships
from its ports were forced to pay protection and customs
duty to those various powers.

By AD 1670, Qatar came under the Bani Khalid tribe's
rule, who had conquered Al Ahsa, in Eastern Arabia, from
the Ottomans. Elsewhere Oman took advantage of Persia's
increasing weakness following its disastrous defeat in
Afghanistan in AD 1711 and occupied Bahrain in

AD1717. However, by AD1736 Persia, under its new ruler Nader Shah Afshar of the new Afshar dynasty, had reoccupied the island, once again bringing the region under Persian domination.

THE START OF QATAR'S MODERN HISTORY

It is following these events, and perhaps as a result of them, that Qatar again has a more defined history and events from this period also resonate in the region's modern politics. In AD 1732 members of the Al Bin Ali family who were part of a tribal federation, the Utub, living in Kuwait, are thought to have settled in what would become Al Zubarah [p125 & p250] in north-west Qatar. Later the Al Khalifa family (who now rule Bahrain), also part of the Utub, moved between AD1762-1768 from Kuwait to Al Zubarah under the leadership of Shaikh Muhammad bin Khalifa. This is the period, which is ascribed to the foundation of the town.

Al Zubarah grew partly because of the instability elsewhere and also because the ruler of the town, Sheikh Mohammad bin Khalifa did not impose customs tax, possibly as he was already wealthy through his own ships and trade. The town developed trading links through The Gulf and attracted traders from Basra, in southern Iraq, to settle in the town after they fled Iraq during the Ottoman – Persian wars between AD 1775/79.

In AD 1782, a skirmish, one of a series, took place on the island of Bahrain between a group from Al Zubarah and Bahraini merchants. The resulting deaths on both sides escalated the incident, and an invasion of Bahrain from Al Zubarah took place, which succeeded in destroying Manama, the main town on Bahrain. Part of their spoils was the ship used by Bahrain's governor to collect customs. In retaliation, plans were made in Bahrain to invade Al Zubarah with 2,000 soldiers being sent from Persia. In May AD 1783 the governor of Bahrain and Busher in Persia, Sheikh Nasr Al-Madhkur, an Omani, sent ships to attack Al Zubarah. They landed away from the town and were defeated by a combined force from the town and surrounding region. Compounding this defeat was an attack on Bahrain, the same day, by Utub tribe members from Kuwait who set fire to Manama. By July AD 1783, Bahrain was captured with a force from Al Zubarah by Shaikh Ahmad bin Muhammad al-Khalifa (the son of Sheikh Muhammed bin Khalifa who was involved in the founding of Al Zubarah), and following that large numbers of people relocated from Al Zubarah to the more easily defended island.

From AD 1787 Al Zubarah came under increasing attacks by the Al Saud family , who then ruled the town of Riyadh in modern Saudi Arabia. In AD 1795 following the capture of Al Ahsa (in eastern modern Saudi Arabia) large numbers of refugees fled from there and arrived in Al Zubarah. Al Saud forces tracked these refugees to Al Zubarah which submitted to the Al Saud and paid tax as protection. Families also moved from Al Ahsa after the seizing of that region in AD 1795 by the Al Saud familyFrom the death in AD 1795 of Shaikh Ahmad bin Muhammad Al-Khalifa in Bahrain, two of his sons jointly ruled Bahrain and Al Zubarah, one son, Sheikh Abdullah bin Ahmed Al Khalifa ruled until 1842. In AD 1797, the Al Khalifa family moved to Bahrain initiating the start of a decline in the fortunes of Al Zubarah. The governor of Al Zubarah, Rahman ibn Jabir Al Jalahima, was tested between AD 1799 and 1802 by a

series of attacks on Bahrain by Omani forces, which
ended after the Al Khalifa, obtained support from the Al
Saud family.

Al Zubarah was the target of a combined attack in AD
1809 by Al Qassimi forces (from Ras Al Khaimah in the
modern UAE) and Al Saud forces, probably in allegiance as
a reaction to increased sea power projected against them
both by Britain and Oman. The town was occupied by
these Al Saud / Al Qassimi forces, giving Britain and
Oman a new conflict centre to consider. In AD 1811, a
combined British / Omani force sailed and attacked Al
Zubarah expelling the Al Saud / Al Qassimi forces and
leaving the town in ruins, the finale of a period of decline
for the town. Britain increased its impact on Qatar when in
AD 1821 an East India Company vessel bombarded the
town of Al Bidda, now part of Doha, as retaliation for what
was said to be piracy committed by its inhabitants. This
action forced between 300 and 400 people to flee from Al
Bidda.

The political result of these conflicts was that from
AD1811 the Al Khalifa family were again the dominant
power in Qatar. In the following years, Britain supported
them through various agreements concerning Bahrain,
notably the General Treaty (which also involved Abu
Dhabi and Ras Al Khaimah) in AD 1820 and a Perpetual
Truce of Peace and Friendship signed in AD 1861. These
agreements were made by Britain to secure The Gulf from
any possible influence by other, non-local, powers especially the French, Ottomans and Russia and later, at the
turn of the 20th Century AD, Germany with their proposed
railway from Berlin, through Baghdad to The Gulf. Subsequent similar treaties, 'Maritime Truces', focused initially
on protecting the pearl trade were signed in AD 1835,

1843 and 1853, these gave rise to the region's name 'The Trucial Coast'.

In AD 1842 an inter-family conflict within the Al Khalifa conflict tried to draw in the Al Saud family and Sheikh Muhammad bin Khalifa Al Khalifa relocated to Al Zubarah. Here he also made allies with Al Jalahima and Al Bin Ali families and then returned to Bahrain where he defeated the ruler of Bahrain and Qatar, Sheikh Abdulla bin Ahmed Al Khalifa. As an indication of how fluid and far-reaching alliances were in the region, Sheikh Abdullah in an attempt to regain his power intended to sail to Zanzibar. He wanted to get the support of Sultan Said Al Said who ruled both Zanzibar and more importantly Oman; however Sheikh Abdulla died on a stop in Muscat.

Al Bidda was destroyed in AD 1847 by Sheikh Mohammed bin Khalifa following the Battle of Fuwayrit and most of the population transferred to Bahrain. These events created a power vacuum in Qatar, and the Al Thani family relocated shortly after from Fuwayrit to the growing settlement of Doha, near Al Bidda.

The Perpetual Truce of Peace and Friendship collapsed in Qatar in AD 1867 following a series of small incidents that culminated in the imprisonment of Sheikh Jassim bin Mohammed Al Thani, the future ruler of Qatar, by Sheikh Mohammed bin Khalifa Al Khalifa. A subsequent battle against Bahraini forces in Qatar lead by the Al Thani family, who were now prominent at that time in Doha was a victory for Qataris. Sheikh Jassim was released in exchange for Bahraini prisoners. Later in the year 24 boats from Bahrain and 70 from Abu Dhabi with a combined total of 2,700 men, attacked Qatar and destroyed the towns of Al Bidda and Al Wakrah. Despite this, Qatari forces were powerful enough to attack Bahrain, destroy 60 boats and kill 1,000 men. This conflict resulted in Britain forcing a change of ruler within Bahrain and the confiscation of all his ships. A substantial fine of $100,000 was levied on Bahrain.

THE LEADERSHIP OF THE AL THANI FAMILY

The British Resident (Minister/Ambassador) in The Gulf, Colonel Lewis Pelly signed a treaty with Sheikh Mohammed bin Thani in AD1868. This treaty represents the acknowledgement of Qatar as a separate entity and the Al Thani family as its leaders.

In AD1871, the Ottoman governor of Bagdad, Midhat Pasha, reoccupied Eastern Arabia following a conflict within the Al Saud family and also occupied Qatar. Despite the alarm of Britain the Ottomans then incorporated Qatar into the *sanjak* (administration area) of Najd (Eastern Arabia) in AD1872. Sheikh Mohammed bin Thani was appointed as the *Qaim-makam* (sub-governor) once again supporting his dominant role in Qatar. In AD1878 his son, Sheikh Jassim bin Mohammed Al Thani, attacked and defeated the residents of Al Zubarah and captured the nearby Al Murair Fort. In the following years, Bahrain once again attempted to regain control of Al Zubarah, probably assuming Britain would support them against the newly confirmed Ottoman *Qaim-makam* Sheikh Jassim bin Mohammed Al Thani; once again Britain did little.

The role of the Ottomans, however, came under pressure because of historical local rivalry. In AD1882 Abu Dhabi occupied Khor Al Udaid, which was at its western limits and the Ottomans would not support the new *Qaim-makam* Sheikh Jassim bin Mohammed Al Thani in regaining it. Sheikh Jassim bin Mohammed Al Thani retali-

ated against the occupation of Khor Al Udaid by raiding
300km south-east of Khor Al Udaid into the Liwa Oasis in
the south-west of the modern UAE; this oasis was the original home of the Abu Dhabi sheikhs.

The almost final conflict between the Ottomans and
Sheikh Jassim bin Mohammed Al Thani followed a
simmering dispute after the Ottoman governor Mehmed
Hafiz Pasha arrived in Qatar from Al Ahsa, with 340-
armed men. Sheikh Jassim bin Mohammed Al Thani relocated to Al Wajbah, 13km west of Doha, with men from
several tribes. After unsuccessful negotiations, the
Ottomans captured and then imprisoned several men on a
ship, the Merrikh. The Battle of Wajbah in AD1893 with
over 4,000 men under Sheikh Jassim bin Mohammed Al
Thani followed . There was a substantial loss on both sides;
however the Qataris defeated the Ottomans, and the result
was that the Ottoman Sultan deposed the governor
Mehmed Hafiz Pasha. This defeat consolidated Sheikh
Jassim bin Mohammed Al Thani's position and reduced
the ability of the Ottomans to govern.

The Ottomans officially renounced sovereignty over
Qatar in 1913 though they remained in Doha until 1915.
On 3rd Nov 1916, Britain signed a protectorate treaty with
Sheikh Abdullah bin Jassim Al Thani where Qatar gave up
independence in foreign affairs in exchange for Britain's
support against external threats; similar agreements had
previously been made throughout The Gulf. Despite this,
Britain continued to have little interest in Qatar's internal
affairs until initial negotiations for oil exploration took place
in 1922.

Oil and natural gas have been a key part of Qatar's
economy for almost 100 years. The Anglo-Persian Oil
Company surveyed in 1926 but no oil was found. After an

oil strike in Bahrain in 1933, a Qatari concession was signed on 17 May 1935 with Anglo-Persian representatives for a period of 75 years in return for 400,000 rupees on signature and 150,000 rupees per annum with royalties with Britain agreeing to provide enhanced security. In October 1938, the first oil well was sunk in Dukhan, on Qatar's west coast, and oil was found in 1939, however due to World War II exports did not begin until 1949.

Over this period, the dispute with Bahrain over Al Zubarah continued, and in 1936 it expanded to include the Hawar Islands, just off the Qatari central west coast. A Bahraini police fort was built on the islands and Bahrain imposed a ban on trade and travel into Qatar. Qatar built Al Zubarah Fort in 1936 as a result of the new Bahraini fort.

The Al Zubarah dispute was settled in March 2001 with a decision by the International Court of Justice whereby Fasht ad Dibal sandbank, Janan Island and Al Zubarah were confirmed as territory of Qatar, while the Hawar Islands and Qitat Jaradah Island were part of Bahrain's territory.

Following Britain's announced withdrawal 'East of Suez', The Gulf sheikhdoms future political situation needed to be addressed by them. For many months, it appeared that Qatar would become part of a union that would include Bahrain and what are now the constituent states of the United Arab Emirates, which includes Abu Dhabi, Qatar's immediate neighbour to the east. Ultimately on 3rd September 1971 Sheikh Khalifa bin Hamad Al Thani, the then Heir Apparent and Prime Minister but soon to be ruler, declared Qatar a separate, independent sovereign state.

In 1971, Qatar also discovered the South Pars/North

Dome Gas Field in The Gulf; this field straddles the maritime border between Iran and Qatar. Production started in 1981 and it eventually turned out to be the largest gas field in the world.

On 27 June 1995, Sheikh Hamad bin Khalifa Al Thani, (known since his abdication as The Father Amir) who is the father of the current ruler Sheikh Tamim assumed power. During his reign the State of Qatar witnessed massive economic, social and cultural development.

In 2002, Qatar hosted the United States Central Command, which in 2009 relocated to its current base at Al Udeid Air Base, west of Qatar.

Sheikh Hamad Bin Khalifa Al Thani abdicated in June 2013 when Sheikh Tamim bin Hamad Al Thani, the current Amir of Qatar, became ruler.

Since 5 June 2017, Saudi Arabia, the UAE, Bahrain and Egypt instated a political and economic blockade against Qatar that has resulted in an increase in the national identity of Qatar.

CHAPTER SEVEN

PEARL DIVING

One of the oldest professions in the Gulf region is pearl diving.

Archaeological evidence dating back to the Late Stone Age in 6000–5000 BC suggest trade and spiritual beliefs in The Gulf included the natural pearl.

The Epic of Gilgamesh a poem from 700 BC Mesopotamia tells that Gilgamesh searched for the "flower of immortality", a well-known early allusion to pearling, by diving using weights attached to his feet. Pliny the Younger, who died in AD 113, wrote about Cleopatra's sumptuous dinner with the Roman general Mark Antony, which included her consuming pearls dissolved in vinegar. Pliny wrote that women in Rome "glory in having these (pearls) suspended from their fingers, or two or three of them dangling from their ears".

The Gulf's pearl industry boomed with increasing stability in the region in the early modern era and its incorporation into international markets. Divers from Oman's Batinah coast and the Yemeni island of Socotra, almost

3,000 kilometres away by sea, came to The Gulf to dive for this valuable resource. By around the middle of the 19th century AD, there can have been few families on the coasts of Eastern Arabia or Western Persia who did not have men working in the pearl business.

Historical records illustrate the extent of pearl diving and the money made. The value of the market in pearl grew over 600% between AD1790 to 1905. Pearls from The Gulf created an income of about US$1.75 million a year from AD1830 risen to US$4 million by the early 20th century.

In the AD1829 book Travels in Assyria, Media and Persia, James Silk Buckingham wrote that pearls from Bahrain brought in approximately £200,000. In the same period, James Wellsted in his AD1838 book Travels in Arabia wrote that there were over 4,000 boats engaged in pearling between Bahrain and Oman.

Pearls from The Gulf were traded to India, the Ottoman Empire, Persia and on to China, Europe and North America, where the aristocratic and emerging middle classes used pearls as luxury items for jewellery and clothing. Sheikh Mohammed bin Thani of Qatar told William Palgrave in AD1877 that: 'We are all from the highest to the lowest slaves of one master, pearl.'

The British Political Resident, John Lorimer, wrote that the industry was worth £625,933 in AD1873/74 and £1,076,793 30 years later in 1904/05 in his Gazetteer of the Persian Gulf. Lorimer also included that there were 350 pearl boats in Doha.

Two species of Molluscs were sought for their pearls. The akoya pearl oysters *Pinctada imbricata fucata*, which grows to a shell length of 60–80 mm and create as a by-product "Lengeh shells" named after the Iranian port, used for products such as buttons. The second and a bigger species *Pinctada margaritifera*, commonly known as the black-lip pearl oyster, which grows to 200 mm in length.

Pearl grounds on the west of The Gulf from Kuwait to Musandam in Oman. They also ran along nearly the whole coast of the Persian side of The Gulf, from near Bushehr (opposite Kuwait) to Lengeh (opposite Musandam) in the south.

Diving for pearls was a seasonal activity from June to September with two diving seasons: the big dive, a 60-day journey, and the small dive, a 40-day trip. Both seasons fell between June and September. Each season dozens of pearling boats left Doha for coastal banks rich with oysters.

The captain, called the *nakuda*, was in command of the whole operation including the pearl divers, *ghawas al lulu*. On the diver's fingers and toes were leather protection, *khabbal*, to protect against sharp rocks, shells and dangerous sea creatures. A wooden nose peg, *fitaam*, stopped seawater drowning the man under deep-water pressure, oil-soaked cotton plugs for the ears, a knife to cut the shellfish of the rock and a basket, *dadjin*, to put their catch in.

A diver used two ropes to descend which his assistant, the *saib*, held from the ship. The driver would remain underwater for 60 to 90 seconds, going as deep as 20 metres. Each vessel could have up to 40 divers, with each person diving perhaps 40 times a day. A crew could gather 8,000 pearl oysters a day. In colder waters in The Gulf, some divers greased their body against the cold water, much as ocean swimmers do.

These divers lived on credit given to them by their captain, who owned and operated their boats and kept the crew. Pearl merchants, *tawawish*, in turn advanced loans to boat captains in advance of the diving season. The pearling industry, therefore, functioned on borrowed capital. The captain would collect all the pearls, and after selling them to the pearl merchant, he would pay the divers in cash, though despite them risking their lives they received the smallest proportion of the sale. The system depended on success each season, with financial ruin for everyone down the chain a possibility.

By 1924, however, the region's pearling industry was already falling into rapid decline. A primary factor affecting that decline was the development of the cultured (artificially encouraged growth of the pearl) pearl industry in Japan from 1916, by the entrepreneur Mikimoto Kokichi.

From then the pearl fishing fleets dwindled, and the men travelled elsewhere to look for work, perhaps to Baku, Iraq and Persia where oil was replacing pearling as the engine of the region's economy.

CHAPTER EIGHT

THE AL THANI FAMILY

T he Al Thani family can be traced back to a branch of the Maadhid tribe, part of the tribal confederation Banu Tamim, one of the largest in Arabia.

From the 17th century AD, the family lived in Ushayqir, a settlement 170km north-west of Riyadh. At some time, they were settled at Yabrin (Jabrin) oasis 280km south-east of Riyadh in present-day Saudi Arabia. During the 18th century AD they moved to the south of Qatar, then to Al Zubarah and then under their leader, Sheikh Mohammed bin

Amir of Qatar Sheikh Tamim bin Hamad Al Thani

Thani, the family eventually settled in Doha around AD 1848. The family takes their name from the father of Sheikh Mohammad, Thani bin Mohammad bin Thamir who died around AD 1860 and was a 14th generation descendent of Maadhid bin Musharaf who lived in Yabrin oasis.

After Sheikh Mohammed's death, his son Sheikh Jassim became ruler in AD1878, developing the pearl trade and expanding trade links to India and East Africa. Sheikh Jassim's accession date on the 18th December is now the National Day for Qatar. Consolidating the rule of the Al Thani family Sheikh Abdullah Bin Jassim Al Thani, who succeeded his father in 1913, signed the Anglo-Qatari Treaty on 3rd November 1913. This treaty followed the Anglo-Ottoman Convention, which resulted in the withdrawal of the Ottoman Sultanate from Qatar. It was under his rule that the first oil well was drilled in Qatar in 1938.

Sheikh Abdullah abdicated in 1949, and his son Sheikh Ali bin Abdullah became ruler. It is from this period that oil was first exported from Qatar, and the subsequent flow of money enabled development in Qatar to accelerate. In 1960, Sheikh Ahmad Bin Ali Al Thani became ruler; during his administration Qatar's independence was declared on 3rd September 1971. The following year Sheikh Khalifa assumed the title of Amir on 22nd February 1972 and ruled until his son, H.H. The Father Amir Sheikh Hamad bin Khalifa Al Thani became ruler in 1995. During Sheikh Hamad's rule, the economy of Qatar grew dramatically with increased oil revenues and the development of Qatar's vast gas fields. Sheikh Hamad was successful in gaining the 2022 World Cup for Qatar.

Sheikh Hamad abdicated on 25th June 2013, and his son His Highness Sheikh Tamim bin Hamad Al Thani became Amir of Qatar. Sheikh Tamim bin Hamad Al Thani was born on 3rd June 1980 in Doha, Qatar, and after completing secondary school attended the British military academy for officers at Sandhurst, graduating in 1998.

Sheikh Tamim is a multi-linguist, fluent in English and French, in addition to Arabic. The increasing educational role of the Qatar Foundation has grown under his administration as has Qatar's substantial cultural engagement in areas not only including Qatari culture, but the broader Islamic world.

CHAPTER NINE

EXPLORERS OF QATAR

I n the 20thCentury AD, the description of Qatar by
foreign visitors create a vivid impression of the country.

In January 1904 **Hermann Burchardt**, the
German explorer and photographer, arrived in Doha after
travelling by sea from Kuwait into Al Uqair and overland
via Al Ahsa. He went to the Turkish Fort which was
located south of the Amiri Diwan (a reception and administration complex for the ruler), in between Al Bidda and
Doha where he was "quartered with the Commander, a
major" and described "Three neighbouring towns are
distinguished. Doha, with the garrison, and Al-Bida'a, and
As-Solata. The garrison consisted of 1 *tabur* (an armed unit
of 250 men appx) with two old cannon. Soldiers, military
officers, and administrative officers with their families dwell
in miserable mud houses, and the state of health is not good;
particularly common are eye diseases. At one time scurvy
was also common; better nutrition for the soldiers has elimi-
nated this disease completely". He continued "in reality the

Turkish influence extends no further than the reach of rifles and canon" in the fort.

Robert Cheesman worked in Iraq from 1920-23 as an assistant to Sir Percy Cox, the High Commissioner of Iraq in the British administration. In 1921 Cheesman travelled through Saudi Arabia and, using the port town of Al Uqair in modern Saudi Arabia, he used the organisation of Abdul Aziz Al Qusaibi the ship-owner and the then Sultan Abdulaziz Al Saud. Cheesman boarded a '*Baghala*' type of Dhow, in April near Al Uqair and crisscrossed between the western shore of Qatar and the eastern shore of the Saudi coast in the Gulf of Salwa, describing how shallow the water was as the boat needed to be pushed despite being 1/4 mile (400meters) from shore. He wrote, "Here the Qatar coast is a sandy shore; scrub grows close to the sea and across one to two miles of undulating sand-dunes until the hills are reached, which appear featureless and level-topped, running parallel with the coast and rising from 200 to 300 feet".

CHAPTER TEN

POPULATION AND GDP

During the 21st century, Qatar's population has increased almost as rapidly as its economy.

Year - Pop - Change% - GDP Billions US$ - Change %

2000 - 590,000 - 0% -$17.57
2001 - 608,000 - 3% - $17.53 - 0%
2002 - 624,000 - 3% - $17.36 - 0%
2003 - 653,000 - 5% - $23.53 - 36%
2004 - 715,000 - 9% - $31.73 - 35%
2005 - 820,000 - 15% - $44.53 - 40%
2006 - 978,000 - 19% - $60.88 - 37%
2007 - 1,178,000 - 20% - $79.71 - 31%
2008 - 1,396,000 - 19% - $115.27 - 45%
2009 - 1,598,000 - 14% - $97.79 - 15%
2010 - 1,779,000 - 11% - $125.12 - 28%
2011 - 1,952,000 - 10% - $167.77 - 34%
2012 - 2,109,000 - 8% - $186.83 - 11%
2013 - 2,250,000 - 7% - $198.72 - 6%
2014 - 2,374,000 - 6% - $206.22 - 4%

2015 - 2,481,000 - 5% - $164.64 - MINUS 20%
2016 - 2,569,000 - 4% - $152.45 - MINUS 7%
2017 - 2,639,000 - 3% - $167.60 - 10%

As of mid 2018 the population (in official Qatari figures) was 2,674,320 of which males are 2,015,284 and females 659.036 (mid 2019 figures are appx 2,740,000). This overwhelming skew towards males is a result of the large numbers of single male migrant workers employed for their labour and skills. It is thought that Indian nationals make up 25% of the total, Bangladeshi 12 %, Nepalese 13% and Pilipino around 10%. Nationals of Qatar probably account for less than 13% of the total population, British nationals around 1% and those from the USA lower than 0.5%.

In 2015, the regional break up of population shows Doha, Al Wakrah to its south and Al Dayyan to Doha's north on the central east coast have a combined population of 50% of the total population in Qatar. The east coast band of perhaps 15km inland from the sea from Mesaieed/Al Wakrah to Al Khor/Ras Laffan is by far the main population base. Given that much of Qatar is within 60minutes drive of Al Corniche in Doha, that the country's towns and villages are within the commuter belt of Doha.

Much of this rise in population has been as a result of the economic impetuous provided by natural gas and to a lesser extent oil with massive urban development, large-scale investment projects and rising government expenditure. The increase in wealth and population has been the engine for infrastructure development such as the port, airport, and soon to be metro system. Along with these communication systems, high profile events including the 2006 Asian Games, 2011 Arab Games and upcoming 2022

Football (Soccer) World Cup require an increased work-force. This very substantial rise in demand for labour and skills means that population growth is expected to continue until 2070 when it may reach 3,400,000 and gradually drift slightly low after that.

CHAPTER ELEVEN

AL KHOR الخور -: *Type of Location* TOWN -: ***GPS***
25.680551, 51.496958 -: *Street* - 49 km by road
north of Doha -: *Public Transport if available* - Bus 102,
102x, 201 & 727 at least every hour between 04:00-23:50
from Al Ghanim Bus Station a 50 minute journey -: *Town /
Area -* الخور -: *Description* - Al Khor is accessed via at least a
three-lane express road. Focused around a sea-lagoon with
patches of Mangrove, there is a variety of natural habitat.
There are a few historical sites, though there are not 'must
see'. The principal one is an old, now closed museum just to
the west of the harbour (GPS 25.686664, 51.512852) and
a series of small watchtowers to the east of the Flag Park
(GPS 25.688401, 51.504425). Within the town are restaurants and accommodation. The town includes housing at Al
Khor Community for Qatar Gas employees along with
other employer-provided communities. Outlying areas
include Al Dhakira and Ash Shafallahiyah. There is a
limited public transport service, on buses 102, 102x, 201 &

727 (at least every hour between 04:00-23:50). -: *Book reference number* 23000

AL RUWAIS الرويس -: *Type of Location* TOWN -: *GPS* 26.131441, 51.20018 -: *Street* - 123km by road north of Doha -: *Public Transport if available* - Bus 100, 101, 201 - at least every hour between 04:10-19:10 from Al Ghanim Bus Station a 90 minute journey -: *Town / Area* - الرويس -: *Description* - Near Qatar's northern tip, Al Ruwais is a port town whose port principally serves to receive regional cargo, which was established in 2011 to replace the now abandoned old port in the town's south, has substantially increased since the Gulf Chris. To the north are sandbar type islands and along the coast are several ruined towns including, Al Jamal, Al Khuwair, and 24kilometres southwest, Al Zubarah. The older town is just to the modern ports east, with Mangrove to the towns east. Offshore are usually dozens of small fishing boats. There is a single hotel and a choice of budget restaurants. -: *Book reference number* 23002

AL WAKRAH (also Al Wakra) الوكرة **(and associated town of AL WUKAIR)** -: *Type of Location* TOWN -: *GPS* 25.177193, 51.604677 -: *Street* - 17km by road south of Doha -: *Public Transport if available* - Bus 109, 119, 129 serving the main road at least every half hour from Al Ghanim Bus Station for the 35 minute journey - and to the souq it's a 1500metres walk. Metro Al Wakrah on the Red Line, though as with the buses it's a long 3-kilometre walk to the souq. -: *Town / Area* - الوكرة -: *Description* - Al Wakrah (also Al Wakra) is one of the older settlements in Qatar, dating to at least 1845; today is it being rapidly subsumed by Doha. The historic trade as with so many coastal towns in Qatar was pearling, with a reported 300 ships by USA Hydrographic Office in the 1920s. Today the population is around 80,000, and it operates mainly as a dormitory for Doha or Mesaieed suggested by the 75% of its population being male. The principal attraction in the town is Al Waqrah Souq a similar development to Souq Waqif in Doha, with any old buildings being restored and the majority of the souq is a modern construction. The waterfront here runs from the small port, north for more than two kilometres past a public park. Immediately in front of Al Wakrah Souq, the sea has been dredged to improve the beach and increase the depth of the water; however, beyond the souq the sea is extremely shallow with sandbanks exposed at low tide for around 500 metres. To the west of the souq and Al Wakrah Main St is Al Wakrah Fort a scenic, though not open to the public, early 20th-century building. West of Al Wakrah, Al Wukair is a small scattered settlement whose slightly older heart is now ringed by 21st-century housing. -: *Book reference number* 23004

Doha

DOHA الدوحة -: *Type of Location* TOWN -: *GPS* 25.29136, 51.533662 -: *Street* - -: *Public Transport if available* - -: *Town / Area* - الدوحة -: *Description* - By far the largest city in Qatar, and probably all the other towns largely serve as an outlier or commercial arm of Doha. Most of Qatar's key attractions are in Doha, including Souq Waqif, Museum of Islamic Arts and National Museum. A reasonable public transport service that will occur following the opening of the Metro makes key attractions easy to get to at low cost. Doha serves as a hub and spoke centre for bus services to other towns. -: *Book reference number* 23006

DUKHAN دخان -: *Type of Location* TOWN -: *GPS* 25.420181, 50.794562 -: *Street* - 84km by road west of Doha -: *Public Transport if available* - Bus 104, 104a,137, 137a at least every hour from 04:30-20:30 from Al Ghanim Bus Station for the 90 minute journey -: *Town / Area* - دخان -: *Description* - Dukhan is a 2nd World War town, established to service the nearby oil fields. As a 'company town', access is against a permit. The area to its north includes Zekreet and the area around 'Film City'. -: *Book reference number* 23008

MESAIEED (Also Umm Said) مسيعيد -: *Type of Location* TOWN -: *GPS* 24.990575, 51.54904 -: *Street* - 38 km by road south of Doha -: *Public Transport if available* - Bus 109 every half hour from 04:09-23:09 from Al Ghanim Bus Station a 90 minute journey -: *Town / Area* - مسيعيد -: *Description* - This is a major town founded after the 2nd World War. It's an industrial centre, receiving piped crude oil from Dukhan and gas from Ras Laffan and islands near Idd Al Shargi. This energy flow supports Fertilizer, Steel and Aluminium plants. A major artificial industrial port services exports. The town has substantial housing projects within it, enabling much of the workforce to have a short commute. Recreational facilities include cricket & football, and there are restaurants though the closest hotels are in Sealine and Al Wakrah, about 20 kilometres north or south of Mesaieed. -: *Book reference number* 23010

RAS LAFFAN رأس لفان -: *Type of Location* TOWN -: ***GPS*** 25.892801, 51.560523 -: *Street* - 83 Km by road north of Doha -: *Public Transport if available* - No public transport -: *Town / Area* - رأس لفان -: *Description* - Ras Laffan is a major industrial development, 66 kilometres north of Doha. It is the major employer in northern Qatar and forms part of Qatar massive energy resource. To its north-west is Al Jassasiya's Rock Carvings. -: *Book reference number* 23012

CHAPTER TWELVE

GOVERNMENT

Q atar is a Monarchy whose head of state bears the title of Amir (sometimes spelt Emir) and honorific title Sheikh.

Unlike the United Kingdom and the United States of America, the head of state in Qatar is to be treated, written and talked about with considerable respect, as considered from within the very deferential Qatari society. The Amir is also executive head of the Government policies & function and commander of the Armed Forces.

A Prime Minister chairs the Council of Ministers; their Ministries deal with their respective functions. Other Government and semi-government bodies also administer and execute the policies of Government.

There is a Consultative Assembly, established in 1972, with 45 members who act as individuals rather than members of a political party (which are not permitted), nominally 30 are elected and 15 appointed. There are both male and female members. Female and male Qatari nationals aged 18years and older can vote.

CHAPTER THIRTEEN

ECONOMY

Qatar's oil and natural gas resources are the country's main economic engine and government revenue source, they comprise 60% of GDP 85% of exports 70% of total government revenue (depending on the fluctuations of oil and gas prices).

Government spending, therefore, drives Qatar's high economic growth and per capita income levels. Robust state spending on public entitlements and booming construction spending, particularly as Qatar prepares to host the World Cup in 2022, looks set to maintain overall economic growth for many years. Although the government has high capital spending levels for ongoing infrastructure projects, lower oil and natural gas prices in recent years have led the Qatari Government to tighten some spending to help stem its budget deficit.

Country - GDP$ - GDP$ per person
Qatar - 193 billion - 70,797
Luxembourg - 62 billion - 104,080
Switzerland - 672 billion - 78,966

United States - 20,351 billion - 62,001
United Kingdom - 2,543 billion - 38,254
UAE - 435 billion - 41,772
Saudi Arabia - 740 billion - 22,411

Looking at the GDP per person figures in The Gulf, they include the very low paid immigrant worker and the fact that a wage-earning Qatari person will often have more non-working children than a person in the UK or USA.

The profit income from oil and gas flow into the government, making the Government the critical engine of expenditure.

Budget
2018 Billion $ - 2019 Billion $ - % change
48.10 - 57.96 - 20.5%
Total expenditure
55.82 - 56.78 - 1.7%
Surplus/Deficit
-28.1 - + 4.3
2018 Billion $ - 2019 Billion $ - % change
Government employees Salaries and Wages
14.36 - 15.68 - 9.40%
Current Expenditure
14.72 - 15.41 - 4.40%
Small projects
1.23 - 1.07 - minus 13.30%
Major Projects
25.52 - 24.61 - minus 3.60%
Total Expenditure
55.82 - 56.78 - 1.70%
Projects in 2019 include
Billions of USDollars
Health
6.236264

Education

5.274725

Infrastructure

9.065934

Housing

3.296703

Transport

4.505495

Qatar's reliance on oil and natural gas is likely to remain for the foreseeable future. Proved natural gas reserves exceed 25 trillion cubic meters - 13% of the world's total and the third largest in the world. Proved oil reserves exceed 25 billion barrels, allowing production to continue at current levels for about 50 years. Despite the dominance of oil and natural gas, Qatar has made significant gains in strengthening non-oil sectors, such as manufacturing, construction, and financial services, leading non-oil GDP to rise in recent years towards half the total.

The major industrial area is Mesaieed Industrial Area south of Al Wakrah. The primary industries here are based on the utilisation of Qatar's oil and gas with Qatar Petroleum, a refinery, lubricants, fertiliser(as a joint venture with by Norsk Hydro using gas as a raw material), fuel additives, vinyl, and chemicals. Using gas as an energy source are aluminium and steel smelters (another joint venture with Norsk Hydro). A major electricity production unit uses natural gas as a power supply. Construction aggregate is both locally sourced and imported, for example gabbro, an ingenious rock similar to basalt, is imported from Oman. North of Mesaieed is the new Hamad Port, a man-made commercial container port, coastguard and adjacent military port constructed from 2010 in an area of *sabka*. It will deal in general containers, vehicles, imported grain and livestock. North of this is a port and commercial district, Um Alhoul, to support smaller scale manufacturing, warehousing & logistics, business services and commercial – retail, services, offices and it will offer hotels. Um Alhoul also is home to a major electricity and water desalination plant that will produce 2.52GW electricity and 514 million litres, per day.

North of Doha is Ras Laffan which is Qatar's original petrochemical complex, supporting several natural gas liquefaction (LNG) plants. Ras Laffan is Qatar's export facility for LNG from Qatar's North Field.

Qatar is also focusing on economic diversification. Transport with a focus on air routes served through Hamad International Airport, supports the development of Qatar as an international communications hub. Qatar Airways with 197 passenger jets and 23 cargo only jets, uses the airport as its hub and spoke centre serving 83 countries and 146 destinations. Tourism is also a partner to the Airport and Airline development.

Tourism is a significant focus of diversification. The number of visitors is planned to increase from 2.9million in 2016 to 5.6million in 2023, grow expenditure from USDollars Billion 4.75 in 2016 to USDollars Billion 10.99 in 2023, an increase in direct contribution to GDP from 3.5% to 4%. Supporting this is an ongoing major redevelopment of Doha Port adjacent to the Museum of Islamic Arts.

CHAPTER FOURTEEN

OIL & GAS

The history of exploration for oil in Qatar is inextricably linked with oil exploration generally in the Middle East.

Qatar is within the historical commercial contract called the 'Red Line Agreement'. This 'Red Line Agreement' grew from an arrangement by Calouste Gulbenkian, an exceptionally well connected Armenian born in Turkey of British citizenship, and the Ottoman Sultan Abdul Hamid II, who had just ascended to the throne. Under it, land available for exploration was transferred from Ottoman government ownership to the Sultan's personal control, the 'Liste Civile', which nullified previous exploration agreements. Over time, German interests obtained small concessions from him in modern Iraq. Most of the territory in adjacent Persia had been signed for exploration under a 1901 agreement with a Briton, William K. D'Arcy, who later unsuccessfully also sought exploration rights within Ottoman domains. The competing interests succeeded in creating an impasse in exploration for oil.

The Young Turk revolution in 1908 altered the economic situation in favour of British interests. In 1910, the National Bank of Turkey was established to support British interests in the Ottoman Empire with Calouste Gulbenkian as a director. He negotiated an agreement between various interested parties and in 1912 Turkish Petroleum Co was founded with shares allocated as 25% Deutsche Bank (which was also involved in the Baghdad Railway project), 25% by a subsidiary of Shell (Anglo-Saxon Petroleum) and 50% for National Bank of Turkey, of which Gulbenkian controlled 15%, excluded was D'Arcy. The outcome of the agreement was a non-compete clause that the partners would only work in cooperation with each other within the territory agreed, in effect a form of cartel. The territorial boundaries of the agreement were formed when a map was produced with a red line drawn through it marking the boundaries of the concession area. The line ran from Turkey to the south, covering the Levant, Iraq and the Arabian Peninsula (except Kuwait). This agreement collapsed after World War II and the establishment of Saudi Arabia.

Despite all this manoeuvring, no company was granted an exploration agreement. Finally, it was agreed that D'Arcy (then known as Anglo-Persian) would obtain 47.5% of Turkish Petroleum Co, Deutsche Bank 25%, Anglo-Saxon Petroleum Co would obtain 22.5%, and Calouste Gulbenkian would receive 5%, after which he became known as 'Mr 5%'. Shortly after this, the Ministry of Finance in Turkey granted a concession lease. World War I paused final negotiations and also resulted in German shares being transferred to the French Government's Compagnie Francaise des Petroles.

The cessation of war in 1918 also resulted in the

United States of America wanting to obtain oil exploration rights in the region, with several USA companies co-operating as the 'Near East Development Corporation' NEDC. During several years of negotiations an eventual agreement was reached that the USA could join the cartel with shares for Anglo-Persian Oil Company, Royal Dutch/Shell, the Compagnie Francaise des Petroles and NEDC at 23.75 % each and Gulbenkian at 5%; the agreement was signed in July 1928 and the company named Petroleum Concessions Ltd. Qatar was included through a new subsidiary, Qatar Petroleum Co.

In Qatar, the initial negotiations for exploration took place in 1922. The Anglo-Persian Oil Company surveyed in 1926, but no oil was found. After an oil discovery in Bahrain in 1933, a further concession was signed on 17 May 1935 with Anglo-Persian representatives for 75 years in return for 400,000 rupees on signature and 150,000 rupees per annum with royalties; Britain agreed to provide enhanced security. In October 1938, the first oil well was sunk in Dukhan and oil was found in 1939, however due to World War II exports did not begin until 1949.

Though labour for the oil industry in Qatar initially was foreign, during the early 1950s Qatari nationals were increasingly employed. This increase in the number of Qatari nationals being employed in the oil industry resulted in improved labour rights and higher wages for the workforce.

Offshore oil was explored by the International Marine Oil Company, and Shell Qatar acquired these fields in 1952. Following this oil was discovered in 1960 at Idd Al Shaqi, (the concession was later acquired by Occidental Petroleum of Qatar). These offshore fields store and export their oil from Halul Island, just under 100km north-east of Doha which was developed by 1966.

Qatar joined OPEC in 1961, a year after the organisation was formed. In 1973, the Qatari government obtained 25% of the shares in Qatar Petroleum Co and in February 1977, the company became wholly owned by Qatar's government.

In 1971, Qatar discovered the **South Pars/North Dome Gas** Field in The Gulf; the field straddled the maritime border between Iran and Qatar. Production started in 1981 in which, eventually, turned out to be the largest gas field in the world. Since 2007, the UAE and Oman share 21billion cubic meters of gas annually from these fields via the Dolphin Gas Project, which was established in 1999.

The Qatar Government withdraw from OPEC on 1st January 2019, explaining that it wished to increase gas production by 43%. Oil production in Qatar is some 1,620,000 barrels per day and 175, Billion cubic meters of gas a year.

CHAPTER FIFTEEN

CULTURE

Q atar is full of contrasts, jaw-droppingly modern, yet deeply conservative; remarkably insular yet potentially open.

Although most people living in Qatar are not Qatari nationals, this section gives an overview of Qatari nationals unless noted otherwise.

There are two fundamental, almost inextricably linked, areas in Qatar that impact its culture, the role of religion Islam and that of the family both nuclear and extended.

The Qatari nuclear family, grandparents, parents and children, forms the key social unit in Qatar. The extended family, which includes first cousins and other cousins, creates further units and the tribe offers form of identity that will be known to other nationals.

Marriages are generally made with the agreement of the parents of both the husband and wife and in a substantial proportion of marriages, it has been arraigned or organised by the family. Marriage is most likely to be from within the extended family with consanguineous marriage as reported within a Qatari Government Ministry of Development Planning and Statistics (MDPS) 2016 statistics report. This report shows these consanguineous figures at 42% with 24% of the total as first cousins. Typically, according to the MDPS report, male Qataris are 26 when they first marry, and females are 24. Polygynous marriage is permitted in Qatar, and the MDPS figures show 8 % of marriages were polygynous. Fertility rates (the number of children a woman has during her life) has declined from four in 2007 to three in 2016, according to MDPS.

Traditionally, socialising takes place from within the extended nuclear family, with male members and female members forming separate groups during the week, usually after working hours if they work. Social activity during the week centres on coffee shops and modern malls, along with informal groups in parks and beaches side locations.

At weekends, the nuclear family is the focus, though as can be imagined first cousins of both a husband and wife may be included as they are also the brother or sister of a spouse.

The tribe is a major source of an individual's identity in Qatar. A tribe is a group of people who share a common identity that, in a simple essence, is the belief they are descended from a single man, and by implication, his wives. It may be that a tribe is a historical accretion of smaller units which today share a collective identity.

Names & titles

Historically the head of a tribe and also major sections within a larger tribe will have the honorific/title Sheikh (a daughter or wife will be a Sheikha, which might also be a given first name, in which case check what is the family name to see which of the two possibilities you have). In Qatar this title is now reserved exclusively for members of the ruling Al Thani family. The title Amir, which means, in this example, prince, reserved for the ruler. A Tribe's members may have the tribal name as their family name/surname, for example, Al Kubaisi (Al means 'the', one of the members of the tribe). A member of this tribe might be called Mohammed bin Ali bin Abdullah; here his first name, Mohammed, is followed by *'bin'* which means son (of), Ali (his father) who is the son of Abdullah, who therefore is Mohammed's Grandfather. A female has a similar name line-up, for example, Sheikha bint Ali bin Abdullah Al Kubaisi (or correctly Al Kubaisia (a feminine ending) ; here the first name is Sheikha (often used as a female first name) bint Ali, the word *'bint'* means daughter (of Ali). On marriage, both the man and woman retain their birth names; however, children have their first name, followed by their father's name and so on.

MARRIAGE

Marriages are often regarded as an agreement between the bride's and groom's families and a contract, *Melcha* (*Milka*), is drawn up and witnesses by suitable people, including the Imam (religious leader) of the major local mosque. Typically, a dowry is paid by the male's family to the female's, after agreement what it should be.

A celebratory event *Shabka* might be held by the families for gifts to be presented. This celebration is followed by agreeing on the date for the marriage, which might be weeks or months away. Before the actual night of the wedding, a *'henna* party' may be held for the females of the families, often nowadays in a hall specially built for weddings or hotel's ballroom (if the hotel is alcohol-free). An event on the night of the marriage is held; the bride and females will have a separate venue from the groom and men. For the bride's party only female guests can attend, perhaps with a strict no camera rule, however as guests will receive a gift the memory will be enhanced. At all celebratory events, the chief participants are at one end of the room and guests always formally greet them.

The men's event is complete with sword dancing and traditional music until, perhaps in a chain of hooting cars, the men's party leads the groom to his new bride. After marriage, typically at least one of the male children and his wife and family will remain living with his parents

Town and Country

There are two intermingling cultures in Qatar; a *bedouin* one, which is the traditional nomadic society where historically a tribe may have had a territory, which was acknowledged as their collective land within which other people could enter with permission. Traits such as bravery alongside generosity epitomised though hospitality is core to the culture of *bedouins*. Alongside this culture is that of the *hadhr,* which is a culture of settled people, in Qatar this is mainly on the coast. The fixed location for these families allowed for educational establishments to develop. However although the family was settled, male members might be away for weeks, months or occasionally years at a time as they worked in pearling or commerce overseas. This obliged women to be involved in many areas in society that men might have otherwise occupied.

Social Greetings

Greetings between members of the same sex is a matter of tradition, perhaps a 'cheek kiss', once on each cheek if you know of each other, maybe twice on the same cheek if you are more than acquaintances, a multiplicity if you are friends and haven't seen each other for a long time. A nose kiss may be given if they are perhaps from the same family. Occasionally a person may kiss the forehead of another person; this is a sign of deference to that other person. Usually during these greetings the right hand is held, or the right hand is placed on the left shoulder of the other person.

Verbal greetings in Qatar are often formulaic and lengthy. Qataris make enquiries the other person's health and family, and the other person reciprocates these. If between men, these enquiries are never about a man's wife, as this is considered disrespectful.

Between a Qatari and non-Qatari, a normal handshake will be used, perhaps the hand is held for a long time of the people who are friends.

Often, even if you have invited a person or group of people for coffee or a meal, there will be a good-natured disagreement after the meal amongst everyone as to who will have the 'honour' of paying for the meal. Do not misunderstand this, each person will happily pay, especially if you are the only foreigner, however if you have invited people do insist; and accept the reciprocal invitation.

Within most population groupings, decisions are top down, whether in major choice making or in smaller issues such as what restaurant to visit. Where the culture is Arab and to an extent, other Asian cultures, this is the form of decision in many businesses. In businesses and area such as meetings for work, a person is addressed using their university degree type or job title, followed by first name, Engineer Ahmed or His Excellency Khalid. To some extent, this explains some of the importance of achieving certification. It may be that a man is called *abu* Mohammed or *abu* Miriam; *abu* means father, and here he is being acknowledged as a father and also it is an indication that he is known well by the person who addresses him, as they also know his child's name. A similar range of address terms are used for women though the term *umm*, which means mother, is used.

Things that would cause embarrassment and loss of face to a Qatari should absolutely be avoided. Criticism might be given indirectly, circumspectly, and never in front of others to avoid that loss of face, perhaps after seeking advice through a person known to you both who is more senior to the person you want to address.

Pointing with a single finger, making a fist or banging a desk to make a point are not acceptable behaviours. Wearing footwear in a home, showing the soles of the feet (even if covered by socks/tights) or footwear's sole should be avoided; though this is not a critical issue as inevitably in a group somebody's feet will be in the general direction of another person. In very traditional meals, food might be eaten with the hand. Here avoid using the left hand to handle food, as this hand is used for personal cleansing; this still applies even if you are left-handed.

Although conversations between groups of friends and family members include politics and religion, these topics are unlikely to be discussed in front of people they are less familiar with. Indeed, if you are a foreign national in Qatar, conversation about politics and religion should be avoided; discussion about the ruling family should also be circumspect. In all cases, a positive viewpoint is usually the most appropriate attitude.

Interaction between non-family males and females takes places within an environment considered acceptable within Islam. Naturally, there is some variance; however in this area caution is ideal. Culturally it is inappropriate for a female to be alone with an unrelated male, this includes being in a vehicle (clearly taxis are an elastic area where sitting in the rear is best if you are a passenger), elevator, room and so on. These situations should be avoided as misinterpretation can easily be made by either the other person or those who are aware of it.

Greeting members of the opposite sex is also an area where traditions play a role. Physically touching those of a different sex is usually considered inappropriate, for example a male and female would not typically shake each other's hands. In very conservative society, touching flesh between members of the opposite sex is considered an intimate act. In these situations, the female would take the lead in either offering or withdrawing her hand from being shaken, and she should try to assess how conservative the male is. Generally, if you are the female consider the circumstances, if it is a business meeting a handshake might be more appropriate compared to social interaction.

Clothing for both sexes is expected to be modest. Qatari men wear the white *thobe* (in winter it may be a dark colour), either with a small stand up collar (Chairman Mao style or western formal shirt collar), both have cuffed sleeves often worn with cuff-links. The *thobe* is usually tailor-made for the wearer incorporating choice of material quality, shade of material, overall design and fit. Under the *thobe* lightweight long *sirwal* pants are worn and a vest (undershirt). The *ghutra* headdress is usually a heavily starched white cloth (in winter it may be red & white or other design), formed from a square of material and folded once across two corners to form a triangle, the longest edge form the front with the apex of the two shorter edges down the back. It is worn in various styles according to the wearer's preference; very distinctive to Qatar is what is known as a 'cobra' style, which you will know when you see it. Under the *ghutra* is a small *ghafiya* cap that provides some grip for the *ghutra* and stops the hair touching the *ghutra*.

The black circle *agil* of rope on the *ghutra* (often with a long tasselled cord at the back that is very Qatari in style) was in the past used to hobble the front legs of a Camel; some religious men do not wear this on the *ghutra*. The men wear formal sandals, or possibly shoes, and in addition to the cufflinks wear a stylish watch and frequently a pen in the *thobe's* chest pocket. Worn for prestige on special occasions such as weddings, is a *bisht* - a traditional long, white, brown or black lightweight Arabic cloak trimmed in gold thread.

The man's ensemble makes a clear statement of the wearer's identity.

Qatari women typically wear a black cloak *abaya* that is worn over the shoulders and reaches just above the ground. Over her head and covering the hair and neck is a scarf *shayla,* also known as a *hijab*. Under this may well be the latest fashion from Paris, elaborate Lebanese style fashion or only jeans and T-shirt, along with other western style underwear.

For non-Qatari men and women, clothing should not be too transparent, revealing or tight. Normally acceptable for women are loose fitting trousers or knee length skirt/dress with covered shoulders and blouse or sleeved T-Shirt should generally be suitable. Tight 'hot-pants' and 'strappy' top, or tops which reveal the naval, chest or back should not be worn. In general, dress conservatively to avoid unwanted attention. Men should not wear shorts in town and always wear a shirt or T-Shirt of a non-offensive design. Wearing clothing with seemingly innocuous text such as "I Love Dubai", or sports team's clothing whose sponsor is an airline of the nation's boycotting Qatar, these include Emirates and Etihad, is inappropriate given the current political situation. On a public beach, men should not wear Speedo-type swimwear; loose swim-shorts are ideal. Women should never wear a bikini on a public beach. Indeed this could be considered provocative. Private hotel pools are the place to wear Speedo or bikini style swimwear.

Avoid physical sign of affection with members of the opposite sex, even your spouse or older children, and do not kiss, hug or engage in any other display of affection with them in public.

Islam is a crucial part of Qatar's culture. It determines activity during the day due to the importance of prayer times. As has been said, it also is critical in the social interactions of males and females. Clothing and its modesty are also impacted by the religion, even details of how far above a person's ankles a garment should be. The foods that cannot be eaten, such as pork, how an animal should be killed and the views on alcohol are all covered by the Quran or sayings of the Prophet Mohammed.

CHAPTER SIXTEEN

LANGUAGE PHRASES

Below is a simplified range of words and phrases; it doesn't include the various gender-based suffixes and prefixes.

English -transliteration -Arabic

hello -marhaba - مرحبا

how are you - kayf halik - كيف حالك

I am fine -ana bikher - أنا بخير

what's your name?-ma ismik - ما اسمك

my name is -ana ismi - انا إسمي

welcome-ahlan wa sahlan- أهلاً وسهلاً

good morning -sabah alkhair - صباح الخير

good evening -masa alkhair - مساء الخير

yes -naam - نعم

no -laa- لا

welcome/ help yourself - tfadhal - تفضل

thanks -shukran - شكراً

goodbye- maa assalama - مع السلامة

sorry -asif- آسف

please -minfadhlak- من فضلك

about / almost -yaani- يعني

where is the....- ayn al....- ..... اين ال

company- ash sharika الشركة

hospital -mustashfaa- مستشفى

hotel -al funduq- الفندق

restaurant -mataam- مطعم

supermarket -subermarket- سوبر ماركت

museum -mathaf- متحف

this is expensive -haadha ghaali- هذا غالي

no it's cheap -la inaha rakhisa - لا إنها رخيصة.

thobe -thoob- ثوب

ghutra -ghutra - غترة

aqal- agaal-عقال

black cloak (for women) - abaya - عباءة

headscarf (for women) - shayla - شيلة

veil covering face - niqaab - نقاب

face mask - birqa - برقع

furniture - athaath - أثاث

chair - kursi - كرسي

table - attawlah - الطاولة

bed - assirir - السرير

carpet - sajada - سجادة

jewels - mujawharat - مجوهرات

gold - dhahab - ذهب

silver fudha فضة

are these made of real gold - hal hadhih masnuwiat min aldhahab alhaqiqi -

هل هذه مصنوعة من الذهب الحقيقي

vegetables - khdrawaat - خضروات

onion - basila - بصلة

cabbage - alkarnab - الكرنب

tomatoes - tamatim - طماطم

cucumbers - khiar-خيار

radishes - fijul-فجل

beans - faswlaya - فاصوليا

potatoes - bitata - بطاطا

fruits - fawakah - فواكه

watermelon - albatikh - البطيخ

lemon - liamun - ليمون

orange - alburtaqali - البرتقالي

dates - tamar - تمر

banana - mawz - موز

peaches - khukh - خوخ

grapes - aanb - عنب

walnuts - eayn aljamal - عين الجمل

I want to drink - ared an ashrab - أريد أن أشرب.

juice - aasir-عصير

orange juice - aeasir alburtuqal - عصير البرتقال

apple juice - aasir altafahu - عصير التفاح

coffee - qahwa - قهوة

tea - shai - شاي

bread - khobz - خبز

rice - aaruz - أرز

cheese - jbin - جبن

egg - bidha-البيض

how much is a dozen eggs? - kam hu dazinat min albida?

كم هو دزينة من البيض؟

meat (beef) - lahm - لحم

lamb - lahm kharuuf - لحم خروف

chicken - dijaaj - دجاج

fish- samak - سمك

shoes - jooti - جوتي

clothes - malaabis - ملابس
shirt - qamis - قميص
traditional pants - sirwaal - سروال
trousers - bantaloon - بنطلون
suit - badhla - بذلة
a dress - fistan - فستان

CHAPTER SEVENTEEN

RELIGION

In AD628 the Prophet Mohammed sent an envoy Abu Al-Ala'a Al-Hadrami to Munzir ibn Sawa Al Tamimi, the governor for Sassanid Persia of Qatar and the surrounding area .

Similar messages were sent to all rulers of lands abutting the Hijaz, where Mecca and Medina the two core towns under Prophet Mohammed's rule are located. The letter asked for his allegiance to the Islamic faith, which he and some of his subjects did. After more correspondence, Mohammed advised that those who did not become Muslims should pay *Jizya* a tax levied on non-Muslims. After the death of the Prophet Mohammed in AD632, a widespread revolt occurred throughout the Islamic world. Abu Al-Ala'a Al-Hadrami was sent by the new Caliph to defeat the rebels. From this date, Qatar increasingly became an Islamic country, mostly Sunni.

Though Christianity was well established in Qatar during this period, Islam gradually became the dominant religion, and by the 10th century AD, probably the entire country was Islamic.

From AD 1787 and the Al Saud incursions from Riyadh in modern Saudi Arabia, Qatar has increasingly followed the Wahhabi version of Islam that is based on the Hanbali school of Islam. As with Christianity, there are different schools of thought within Islam, which often develop a distinct identity. The Hanbali school follows the law and culture as given in the Quran, the Prophet Mohammed's sayings, customs and records by the companions of the Prophet Mohammed. This approach is much the same way as the Bible, sayings and traditions of Jesus and accounts made by his disciples inform the behaviour of Christians. Unlike other Islamic schools, the Hanbali school does not accept legal or cultural interpretations from those other Islamic schools of thought.

The name Hanbali comes from an Iraqi academic Ahmed bin Hanbal who died in AD 855. This school was followed by Imam Muhammad ibn Abd al-Wahhab, who lived from AD 1703-1792. He was a student of several Hanbali theologians, who espoused ideas at the extreme of Sunni Islamic thought. Imam Muhammad ibn Abd al-Wahhab gained the support of local rulers to the north of what is now Riyadh in modern Saudi Arabia, these eventually included the ruler of a town, Diriyah also near Riyadh, Sheikh Muhammed bin Saud. These two men collaborated to expand their political and religious territory, which by AD 1818 covered large areas of Arabia including the Qatar peninsula but excluding most of Oman and Yemen, the state is now called the First Saudi State. After the fall of this state in AD 1818, a Second Saudi State developed from AD 1824 which further increased the influence of Wahhabism in Qatar.

The basis of Islam is what has been called the **Five Pillars of Islam** that are incumbent on each Muslim.

- *Shahadah* testimony of faith each Muslim must recite in the form: 'There is no God but Allah, and Muhammad is His Prophet'.
- *Zakat* charitable giving
- *Sawm* Fasting during the month of Ramadan.
- Making the *Haj* pilgrimage to Mecca at least once during one's lifetime, if possible.
- *Salat* prayers five times a day.

The mosque is the first and quintessential Islamic building. In Arabic, the name is *masjid* which means "place of prostration". The Prophet Muhammad's house, which was a typical 7th-century AD Arabic style house, with an internal courtyard giving access to the rooms around it acting as the first mosque. The ceilings of the rooms were supported by columns, creating what is now called a hypostyle (meaning under columns) mosque and larger mosques in Arabia followed this style.

The critical function of a mosque is a place of prayer to Allah (God), though it is acceptable to worship elsewhere. Prayers are held five times daily based on solar time, the position of the sun in the sky; therefore the time of worship varies throughout the year and will also depend on the location. The first prayer is about 10 minutes before sunrise; second at solar noon; third late afternoon (initially based on a calculation of the time that a person's shadow became a specific proportion of their height); fourth when the entire solar disk has sunk below the horizon; fifth when, according to some Islamic schools of thought, the sun is between 12 & 18 degrees below the true horizon, this is around 90minutes after the 4th prayer. Today, technology has, fortunately, simplified matters immeasurably.

Imam Muhammad ibn Abd al-Wahhab Mosque

In Islam, it is preferred that for the midday Friday prayers men gather as a community in a *masjid al jumaa* (congregational mosque) with an Imam to lead prayers. Most mosques do not have a particular Imam (prayer leader); however, in urban areas there is a major mosque to serve a district, the *masjid al jumaa*, which does. The word *jumaa*, which in this instance means congregation, comes from the same Arabic 'root' word as for Friday and university. Many of these *masjid al jumaa* are named in memory of an individual, such as Imam Muhammad ibn Abd al-Wahhab Mosque the State Grand Mosque of Qatar.

On entering almost all mosques, a visitor faces the *mihrab* (prayer niche) which faces towards Mecca, which in Qatar is towards the south-west. This direct relationship between a mosque's main entrance and the *mihrab* is the preferred one. Though a mosque's purpose is to accommodate prayers, it is possible to prayer in any clean, respectable place and for that, a small prayer rug can be used, to ensure a clean surface on which to pray. Some major mosques in Qatar have prayer space for women and a mezzanine floor enabling them to hear the prayer service if they attend, without being themselves overlooked by men.

RAMADAN

Ramadan is the holy month, when Muslims abstain from eating, drinking and smoking between sunrise and sunset during the entire month. Non-Muslims are affected because it is prohibited to be seen eating, drinking (in any form) or smoking in public places during daylight hours in Ramadan. As a result, most restaurants are closed (though large hotels main restaurants usually function for non-Muslims), all bars are closed, and hotels are not permitted to serve alcohol publicly. Working hours are shorter, with later starts and earlier finishes. Ramadan is looked forward to and enjoyed by Qataris, as it is a time for self-restraint, spiritual reflection, and visiting friends and family after evening prayers, when social activity tends to go on late at night. During Ramadan, government offices are open from 09:00-14:00, Saturday to Thursday; offices that deal directly with the public will have shorter hours than normal but longer than 09:00-14:00. Banks may work from 10:00-14:00 / 21:00-23:00 (check specific timings). Other businesses and smaller shops will also have altered hours with short timings during the day and later closing at night. Major supermarkets may have unaltered timings. As it follows the lunar calendar, Ramadan moves forwards each year (falls earlier) by about 11 days.

CHAPTER EIGHTEEN

EDUCATION

B efore 1949, Qatar had simple schools that focused on teaching the Quran.

A school for boys was established in Doha in that year because of the increasing income from oil exploration. From then other schools were established in 1954, and the first girl's school started in 1956. By 1976 there were 130 schools in Qatar with an equal split between boys and girls schools.

Today education for Qatari nationals and foreign employees of the education ministry is free. There are three streams of education in Qatar; elementary school for children aged 6 to 12, preparatory school for children aged 12 to 15 and secondary school for children aged 15 to 18. Up to aged 15 education is compulsory. Qatari government schools are single-sex with English taught as a foreign language.

From 1964, there has been a variety of fee-paying International schools in the country, catering primarily for children of non-Qatari nationals, although Qatari's can and do attend. There is a wide variety of national curriculum followed at various grades, including USA (32 schools), UK (131) and Canadian (3). In private schools, the history of Qatar is taught in addition to their national curriculum along with Arabic and Islam if the student in Muslim. Schools may be coeducational or single-sex. The Qatari government supports Qatari nationals attending with up to QAR 28,000 as a grant.

The major Qatari university 'Qatar University' was founded in 1973; there are now seven Qatari university-level educational institutions. Within Qatari government, universities there are scholarships available to non-Qatari nationals. Additionally, there are 19 foreign university-level establishments in Qatar, mainly from the USA, with campuses predominantly at Education City; the first international university was Virginia Commonwealth University. Most of the international academic level establishments offer a limited range of courses based on their parent body supplying material and tutors. There is some segregation of the sexes at classroom level at several universities. Overall, about 65% of students (in both government and private universities) are female with a comparable percentage graduating.

The education system is under the authority of several bodies; the Supreme Education Council which oversees the education system at all levels from pre-school through university; the Ministry of Education which is gradually being subsumed by the Supreme Education Council; finally and in effect an autonomous body the Qatar Foundation (for Education, Science and Community Development) which aims to place Qatar at the cutting edge of Education with an especial emphasis on the inclusion of foreign Universities.

CHAPTER NINETEEN

PUBLIC HOLIDAYS

2020 1st January New Year's Day (banks only, not official government holiday)

2020 12th February National Sports Day. This holiday is on the same date each year.

2020 1st March Early March (banks only, not official government holiday first Sunday in March)

2020 23rd April Ramadhan starts 23 April and finishes 23 May. Dates are dependent on lunar sighting and the start of officially announced, possibly the day before. The end of Ramadhan is dependent on the beginning of Eid Al Fitr

2020 24-26th April Eid Al Fitr, this is an Islamic Holiday and dates are dependent on the new moon sighting and the start is officially announced, possibly the day before. The number of day's holiday are also announced then.

2020 30th July 30 – 1st August - Eid Al Adha, this is an Islamic Holiday and dates are dependent on the new moon sighting and the start is officially announced, possibly the day before. The number of day's holiday are also announced then.

2020 18th December atar National Day – (Founder's Day - public holiday). This is an official holiday on the same date each year.

CHAPTER TWENTY

ARRIVAL INTO QATAR

M any nationalities (46 countries) can obtain a free 30-day tourist visa-waiver on arrival in Qatar, if having a valid passport that should be valid for a minimum period of 6 months from the date of entry into Qatar.

Qatar Airways

The tourist visa-waiver is valid for up to 30 days in Qatar, during either a single trip or on multiple trips. This waiver may be extended for a further 30 days (some nationalities whose country's have reciprocal agreements get longer) https://dohahamadairport.com/airport-guide/at-the-airport/visas-immigration (other nationalities can apply through here

https://qatar.vfsevisa.com/Qatar-Online/QROnline/VisaCategoryAndPricingDetails/ UnRestrictedNationalityList.

When planning your visit to Qatar, consider the impact of the Gulf Crisis on your choice of arrival and departure route. Due to the Gulf Crisis, there are no direct flights from Bahrain, Egypt, Saudi Arabia and UAE; there are also no overflights via these countries for Qatar Air, this impacts arrivals from Europe especially southern Europe, lengthening flight times. If you are travelling around The Gulf on business that includes Qatar, consider Oman as an alternative flight hub as it has three airports served by Qatar Airways and additionally two local airlines operate throughout The Gulf.

Airlines serving Doha include British Airways (Heathrow), Oman Air (Muscat), Pegasus Airlines (Istanbul); Salam Air (Muscat); Qatar Airways (innumerable airports including Austria - Vienna; Australia - Adelaide; Canberra; Melbourne; Sydney; Perth; Belgium - Brussels; Canada - Montréal–Trudeau; China - Hong Kong Shanghai–Pudong; Denmark - Copenhagen; Finland - Helsinki;France - Nice; Paris–Charles de Gaulle; Germany - Berlin–Tegel Frankfurt; Munich;Greece - Athens; India - Mumbai; Ireland - Dublin;Italy - Milan–Malpensa; Pisa ; Venice; Rome–Fiumicino; Japan - Tokyo–Haneda; Tokyo–Narita; Netherlands - Amsterdam; Norway - Oslo–Gardermoen; Poland - Warsaw–Chopin; Portugal - Lisbon; Singapore - Singapore;South Africa - Durban; Cape Town; Spain

- Barcelona; Madrid; Sweden - Gothenburg; Stockholm–Arlanda; Switzerland - Geneva; Zürich; UK - Birmingham; Cardiff; Edinburgh; London–Heathrow; London–Gatwick; Manchester; USA - Boston; Chicago–O'Hare; Dallas/Fort Worth; Houston–Intercontinental; Los Angeles; Miami; New York–JFK; Washington–Dulles.

Allow plenty of time for immigration procedures and especially for emigration. You should also ensure that you have ample time when using transfer services.

For customs, check the airport information https://do-hahamadairport.com/airport-guide/at-the-airport/security-customs. Prohibited items include but are not limited to (for which you should check the official airport information) weapons, firearms and ammunition/ alcoholic beverages/ pork products/ narcotic drugs (other drugs include codeine). If you take prescription drugs, always bring your doctor's prescription. Check with the Qatar embassy in your country for official details.

Many airlines apps not only offer flight information, but also very usefully will update with your checked baggage information including what luggage carousel you should find it on. This app is useful in the unfortunate event that your luggage is delayed, you should know shortly after landing, if you have internet access. Lost property Hamad International Airport: Phone+974 4010 6666/4462 6531

Airport   hialostproperty@hamadairport.com.qa/ llqas@qataraviation.com

Flight   status   https://dohahamadairport.com/air-lines/flight-status

Check with the Qatar embassy in your country for details

Tobacco allowance: 400 cigarettes.

Personal items and gifts up to a maximum value of Qatari Riyals (QAR) 3,000.

Imports of alcohol and narcotics are prohibited.

Inside the luggage area is an information area, ATM machines (ideal as this area is less busy than outside), currency exchange (rates are not as reasonable as those in the city). After immigration and customs, exit immediately into the arrivals hall, which has toilets, information, ATM machines, phone company outlet, currency exchange, lost property and coffee shops.

Inter-Terminal Transfer

There is an automatic shuttle Metro within Hamad International Airport, connecting the north & south nodes of the airport.

METRO

The Doha Metro system's the Red Line, also known as the Coast Line, has three termini including **Hamad International Airport.** The metro connects the airport with Msheireb interchange near Souq Waqif and onward to other stations including West Bay and Legtaifiya near The Pearl (about a 30minute journey). A full day pass is QAR6/-.

MOWASALAT Bus Services

The Mowasalat Bus Station 25.259431, 51.612566 at Hamad International Airport is signed west (turn right after you exit immigration) of the arrival area.

Bus 737 timings 24 Hours from Airport to Al Marat St (west outside City Centre Mall)

Bus 757 timings 24 Hours from Airport to Al Mansoura St (in general area of City Centre Mall)

Bus 777 schedule 05:00-24:00 from Airport to West Bay (City Centre Mall) and The Pearl via Corniche

Bus 109 timings 04:04-23:04 from Airport south to Mesaieed (via Al Wakrah south of Doha) and north near Souq Waqif (in city centre) check direction of the bus.

Bus 747 timings 04:42-23:42 from Airport to Souq Waqif near Corniche (travelling near Al Ghanim Bus Station and many hotels)

Bus 727 timings 04:00-23:50 from Airport to Al Khor (north of Doha - skirting far west of city centre on D Ring Road)

These bus routes are less than QAR7 and must be paid with exact change or with a KARWA smart-card (tap on boarding the bus and tap on exit). Buy the KARWA card at ticket vending machines at Hamad International Airport, Al Ghanim Bus Station, The Pearl Qatar and Qatar Mall. Cost QAR30 valid long term and can be topped up; QAR20 unlimited journeys in 24hours; QAR10 for two trips in 24hours.

Immediately outside the south exit (straight after immigration) are the hotel buses for complimentary services.

TAXI

From the Airport you can obtain Mowasalat car services For Taxi Bookings 800-TAXI (8294) +974 800 8294 (reduced mobility +9744458 8888 with advance notice 48hours+ ideal), For Limo Reservations 800-LIMO (5466) (+974) 800 5466 (taxi rank is to the east outside arrivals from gate number 2 or 3) or download Karwa app (and ensure you have your exact location entered on Map by GPS - if needed do it manually). Uber is available. Fares Airport to Souq Waqif up to QAR45 and The Pearl up to QAR75 (for luxury) – traffic in the city centre can, of course, add to these costs. Careem taxi (app available) a Gulf-wide taxi service offers a comparable service and fares to Uber, for example, Careem G+ Airport – Souq Waqif GO+ 35 and Airport to The Pearl G+ QAR55.

In all app hailed taxi services the app is your payment system and cash, even if requested by the driver as might happen, is not a substitute and may lead to double payment or issues regarding your payment.

CAR HIRE

There are about 20 car rental services available at the Airport exit south of arrivals (immediately ahead - and it's on the other side of the road with pedestrian crossings available), including

Europcar   www.europcarqatar.com/;   Avis www.avisqatar.com/;Hertz   www.hertz.-com/rentacar/reservation/;And local including Al Mana (a major group) http://www.almanaleasing.com/; Mustafawi http://www.mustafawi.qa/;   Strong   (http://www.strong-rentacar.com/) Rates are from QAR100/ per day.

If you use an international car-hire company, consider downloading their app, which may make any booking a better experience.

To rent a car for up to seven days from several countries, including the EU / USA, your full driving licence should be acceptable, with suitable validity of vehicle type and period validity. For more than seven days, you will need an International driving licence or a license issued from a GCC (Gulf Cooperation Council) country. Also required will be your credit card with a minimum of three months validity; your Passport will be photocopied, and fines will be payable before departure. Ensure you know exactly where to return the car as the staff need quick access to the vehicle to charge you (the location is usually the short-stay – check which one (there are west and east –

both on three levels and note that Qatar Airways and other airlines are in different locations within the airport).

Ensure you are familiar with the operation and safety features of the vehicle you will drive, ask the hire office staff; this is especially important if you will drive off-road with a 4x4.

5*hotel information desks are available; exit south of arrivals (immediately ahead - and it is on the other side of the road over the pedestrian crossings) and here you can obtain hotel shuttle bus services.

MOBILE PHONE

There are two mobile phone (cell phone) operators in Qatar on the GSM system, Ooredoo and Vodafone. SIM cards can be obtained against presentation of ID documents (passport if a visitor), with pre-paid varieties available; look for the appropriate outlet in the airport or elsewhere such as shopping malls. Top-up cards (QAR from 5 - 200) are widely available throughout the country and can offer a talk, text and internet usage. There are various types of top-up card available so make certain which one you wish to buy and actually do buy.

ARRIVAL BY SEA

There are Cruise Lines that call into Doha – principally on a circular cruise, similar to a Mediterranean or Caribbean cruise, with Dubai as the terminus. Currently, AIDA, MSC and TUI (Mein Schiff) call variously into Abu Dhabi/Dubai/Oman/Bahrain/Doha in the winter months. Other cruise lines which visit Doha are on around the world cruises, these include Seabourn. In Doha, shore excursions include a short city tour and sand-dune safari.

At the moment, there are no international roads with traffic that enter Qatar due to the Gulf Crisis.

EMBASSIES

Some Qatar embassies overseas

Canada Ottawa (embassy)

http://ottawa.embassy.qa/en

Embassy Qatar

150 Metcalfe Street, 8th floor

Ottawa, Ontario

K2P 1P1

+16132414917

+16132413304

ottawa@mofa.gov.qa

http://ottawa.embassy.qa/en

United States Washington, D.C. (embassy)

Embassy of the State of Qatar

2555 M St, NW

Washington, DC, 20037

+12022741600

+12022370682

washington@mofa.gov.qa

http://washington.embassy.qa/en

United Kingdom London (embassy)

Embassy of the State of Qatar

South Audley Street

W1K 1NB

London - UK

020 7493 2200

london@mofa.gov.qa

http://london.embassy.qa/en/services

Cultural Attaché

21 Hertford Street - London

Tel: 0207 495 8677

Australia Canberra (embassy)

Embassy of the State of Qatar
Q10 Akame Circuit
O'Malley ACT 2606
Canberra – Australia
+61261528888
canberra@mofa.gov.qa
http://canberra.embassy.qa/en
France Paris (embassy)
Embassy of the State of Qatar
1, rue de Tilsitt 75008
Paris France
+33145519071
paris@mofa.gov.qa
http://paris.embassy.qa/en
Germany Berlin (embassy)
Bonn (embassy branch office: medical office)
Embassy of the State of Qatar
Hagenstr 56
14193- Berlin
Germany
+4930862060
berlin@mofa.gov.qa
http://berlin.embassy.qa/en

FOREIGN EMBASSIES IN QATAR

Australia

21st Floor, Tornado Tower
Majlis Al Taawon St
Doha
Qatar
Phone: +974 4007 8500
Fax: +974 4007 8503
Email: embassy.doha@dfat.gov.au

Phone: +974 4007 8500
https://qatar.embassy.gov.au/

Canada
Tornado Tower,
Corner of Majlis Al Taawon Street and Al Funduq Street,
Doha, State of Qatar
Telephone: (974) 4419 9000
Hours of operation
Sunday to Wednesday
8:00 am to 4:30 pm
Thursday
8:00 am to 1:30 pm
E-mail: dohag@international.gc.ca
https://www.canadainternational.gc.ca/qatar/

France
Diplomatic St
West Bay, Diplomatic area,
P.O. BOX: 2669 DOHA
Hours 08:00-16:30 (not Friday)
In case of emergency: (+ 974) 66 84 50 83
Email: contact@ambafrance-qa.org
https://qa.ambafrance.org/-English-

Germany
Fereej Kulaib
Hours 08:00-13:00 (not Friday)
6, Al Jazira Al Arabiya Street
P.O. Box 3064
Doha
Qatar
TELEPHONE(+974) 4408 2300
FAX(+974) 4408 2333

EMAILinfo@doha.diplo.de
https://doha.diplo.de/
United Kingdom
West Bay Dafna Area, Onaiza Zone
66, Al Shabab Street
P.O. Box 3
Doha
Qatar
TELEPHONE(+974) 4496 2000
08.00-15.30 (not Friday)
embassy.doha@fco.gov.uk
consular.dohaa@fco.gov.uk
https://www.gov.uk/world/qatar
United States
U.S. Embassy Doha
22nd February Street
Al Luqta District
P.O. Box 2399
Doha, Qatar
Phone: (974) 4496-6000
Fax: (974) 4488-4298
https://twitter.com/usembassyQatar
https://qa.usembassy.gov/

Check your government's travel advice to Qatar. This advice will update periodically and will have an impact on areas such as holidays booked through travel agents and insurance validity.

https://www.gov.uk/foreign-travel-advice/qatar
https://travel.state.gov/content/travel/en/traveladvisories/traveladvisories/qatar-travel-advisory.html
https://smartraveller.gov.au/countries/middle-east/pages/qatar.aspx

CHILDREN

Qataris love children, so you will find yours get a warm welcome. An important issue for everyone especially children will be sunburn, at any time of year, and heat. If you intend hiring a car or will use a chauffeur drive type, enquire in advance about the availability of child car seats for your children and as always with any service request in Qatar follow this up once confirmed before you arrive. Hotels and restaurants are usually pleased to have children; however high chairs are a rarity, so again if needed factor this into your choice.

CLOTHING

Loose fitting polycotton mix is best as the cotton will absorb sweat, and the man-made fibre helps keep the shape. If you have breathable or fast-dry that's also a good choice as the relatively high humidity will cause you to sweat al lot. For most occasions, when eating out a 'smart casual' is all you will need, it's only in the more formal 5* hotels that you will need to 'button-up'.

Doha has a largely well-paved street network so shoes that you find comfortable to walk around town should be ok. However, out of Doha, in the desert, you will need shoes that can manage with rough loose surfaces. Here sandals are not ideal as they don't protect against toes being hit by stones or thorns and insect bites etc.

OTHER

Qatar will have all the little things you need, such as pharmacies, good doctors, toiletries and personal care, including sanitary towels etc. for women. Prices are broadly comparable to European prices.

POWER

Qatar runs on 240v, and 50Hz electricity supply with

plugs a mix of mainly square 3 Pin with some round 3-Pin; some electrical equipment is sold with a 2-pin plug. The UK is 230v and 50Hz, so Qatar power is usually compatible with UK standards though you may need a socket adaptor. The USA and Canada run on 120v and 60Hz; therefore you will need an adaptor for power and plug sockets. Australia runs on 230v and 50Hz so you will not need a power adaptor but will need an adaptor for plug sockets. Your hotel may have adaptors to for your devices; they certainly are widely available in Doha at low cost.

CHAPTER TWENTY-ONE

HEALTH AND ACCESSIBILITY

The quality of healthcare in Qatar is generally very high.

There are many excellent healthcare providers and well-stocked pharmacies, with English speaking staff, throughout Doha city and beyond, including some which are open 24 hours.

If you travel with medicines, always bring current prescriptions with you to Qatar as surprising medicines, such as Codeine, are on banned import lists and do need evidence of Doctors prescribing them. It's also helpful to show the prescription to a local Qatar healthcare provider should you need additional medicine as you may require a local prescription. Pharmacies in Qatar are well stocked and include the UK Boots brand franchise. Many of your requirements or a suitable substitute should be available at these pharmacies if you run out for any reason.

Ensure you have proper insurance to cover you for medical treatment, making certain you are covered for existing conditions, as you will be required to pay for medical treatment, and emergency evacuation in case of serious accidents needs to be considered. Typical travel health threats need to be considered, such as deep vein thrombosis (DVT).

The temperature and effect of the sun may well be the primary health issue that most visitors will need to consider. In mid-summer, the sun's angle in London is lower than it is in spring or autumn in Qatar, and therefore protection against sunburn should be taken throughout the year; most especially for children. Drinking rehydrating liquids is essential as outside air-conditioned buildings, the heat causes water loss, and inside the drying effect of that air-conditioning will also affect the body's water content. Consider the impact of heat exhaustion and heat stroke if you hike outside, their symptoms including red, dry or damp skin, headache, and dizziness. Water from the tap in Qatar is likely to be safe, certainly to brush teeth etc. In Doha, the water is desalinated seawater that leaves the water desalination station safe to drink, though with a noticeable taste. However travelling through the water-pipe system and perhaps being stored in a tank, does mean that its safety, as in all other countries, may be compromised.

As this book is not an authority on health safety, you should review your own government's travel advice to Qatar, as they are experts in their specific field.

www.fitfortravel.nhs.uk/destinations/middle-east/qatar

https://wwwnc.cdc.gov/travel/destinations/travel-er/none/qatar (note the unique prefix)

It is important to consult with your health care provider about your own personal health requirements and their opinion about your needs when travelling to Qatar as that is the only way to ensure you get the correct advice. They may review hepatitis A; hepatitis B; rabies and tetanus vaccines as options. Your health care provider may also discuss with you how the heat may affect you and how you can be aware of symptoms, especially in younger and older people such as dry skin, muscle cramps, nausea, headaches and confusion, particularly as some medications may increase the effect. Other areas they may discuss, most especially in younger and older people who are more vulnerable to viral and other health issues, might include preventing contracting leishmaniosis, which is spread by sand flies, which can cause itchy bumps or rash and lesions and glands swelling. Other insect-spread issues they may discuss are malaria and dengue fever and West Nile virus, which are spread by mosquitos. Ask your healthcare provider about their recommendation to repel insects, including the effectiveness and suitability for you of Deet and Permethrin if you will travel outside towns in Qatar. Some health providers may mention rabies, MERS-CoV virus (a camel spread infection, including through drinking un-pasteurised camel milk) that is related to SARS pneumonia and Crimean-Congo haemorrhagic fever (a tick-spread disease), though the incidence of these is very low.

Check also with your government or with www.masta-travel-health.com or www.passporthealthusa.com for vaccinations.

Special Needs Travellers

Though a modern country, Qatar does not have the range of facilities required by many travellers with special needs. Speak with your health-care provider and specialised organisation for their knowledgeable advice in your particular instance. There are some low floor buses with designated seating for people with special needs, however, most buses do not have these. Major shopping malls and 5* hotels will have the best facilities; many have lifts and broad corridors and, critically, special needs toilets. Souq Waqif has reasonable accessibility, and special needs toilets, however the uneven 'ancient' streets might cause problems. The Museum of Islamic Arts has good access and wide corridors in galleries and special needs toilets. The National Museum is very much worthwhile visiting and again has good access and wide corridors in galleries and special needs toilets. Mathaf Museum has reasonable access, some steps on the outside, along with special needs toilets. Most other museums have limited facilities. The Corniche has a reasonable surface along with very wide pedestrian access. Camel race tracks and other sports facilities have limited access.

Q atar, for most visitors and residents, is a safe country, with few physical assaults or robberies.

In general, safety standards are comparable to most western countries. However a 'health and safety' style of passive safety features is less common, and therefore you should be more alert regarding your immediate environment and the impact it may have on your safety.

Having appropriate insurance when you visit Qatar is important and do remember to note all possible health issues to have or have had. Insurance is especially important as third-party liability within Qatar is adjudicated under a very different legal system to many western countries. Any claims awarded in Qatar that are successful may attract a very much smaller monetary compensation than in most western countries. Claims against you, in the event you are liable, are also likely to attract lower financial payment, except if an accident results in death. Your insurance policy should include air-ambulance repatriation.

As this book is not an authority on foreign safety, you

should review your own government's travel advice to Qatar.

https://www.gov.uk/foreign-travel-advice/qatar

https://travel.state.gov/content/travel/en/traveladvisories/traveladvisories/qatar-travel-advisory.html

The use and handling of your Credit card should be examined to ensure its security, as you would do within your own country, most particularly in public places and if handled by third-parties. Do advise your bank that you will be travelling in Qatar to ensure that it can be used. Personal belongings, most especially those of value such as passports, should be held in a safe and secure place including when travelling to your destination. Copies of essential items should be made and then stored in a location separate from the original.

Severe penalties are carried out for possession & use of prohibited drugs, as does trafficking in them which if a person is convicted can carry the death penalty. Drinking alcohol in public and in non-designated locations (designated locations include restaurants serving alcohol) is also prohibited. Alcohol may not be carried into Qatar, there is however a duty-free at the airport, enabling you to buy alcohol on departure.

Using abusive language or making rude gestures are actions that may result in your arrest. Demonstrations of affection, such as kissing in public, should be avoided as, if an influential person takes offence, the police may be called.

Homosexual acts carry potentially severe penalties in Qatar, including several years in jail. Consider that public homosexual sexual activity will bring a higher punishment than for heterosexual. Additionally, 'cross-dressing' in the case of men is likely to result in arrest. Sharing a twin-bed room with a person of the same sex is a normal practice in the region, as a cost-saving choice, so will not attract any undue attention unless you invite guests. Do review your own government's advice.

Pornography is prohibited, and the internet is very effectively monitored and censored.

You own government is unlikely to be able to offer more than basic advice about lawyers who can act for you if you are arrested, prosecuted or jailed.

The most common safety impact on individuals is by road traffic, including dangerous driving, both within urban areas and out-of-town. If you drive, adopt a mode of 'defensive driving', most especially staying alert when in Doha. Ensure you wear seat belts, and that suitable additions are available for children. Outside Doha, straying animals may be encountered on roads, and these add to dangers when driving. Off-road driving increases the risk in all respects, especially at speed. Pedestrians should also remain alert and try to walk facing the traffic so that awareness of oncoming vehicles is possible.

CHAPTER TWENTY-THREE

INTERNAL TRANSPORT

E xcept in limited areas like Souq Waqif, Al Corniche, The Pearl and Katara, Doha is not a city to walk in, main roads have few crossing options and even in winter the temperature, for many visitors, precludes walking any distance.

Internal transport in Qatar is supported by a reasonably well-maintained network of roads, several app-based taxi options, bus routes and new soon to open metro and tram system in Doha.

Driving

Qatar drives on the right-hand side of the road (as in USA and much of the world). There is a mix of traffic light controlled road junctions, roundabouts (*rotary*) and flyovers. Signage's text is in Arabic and English with speed and distance signs in kilometres with numbers only in the Hindu/Arabic number system (as used in the west). Vehicles are typically automatic, with large engines and air-conditioning. In essence driving regulations are comparable to most western countries, including not leaving the scene of an accident (see below), fines for illegal parking, penalties for not wearing seat belts, using phones etc. The maximum speed is 120kmph, with lower speeds in places down to 60kmph. There are some 100 petrol stations in Qatar, offering a variety of services, including shops and car wash. Petrol (gasoline/fuel) prices are set by the government and recently have varied between QAR 1.55 – 1.80 per litre. Service is by an attendant, and they are low paid, so a small tip/rounding up helps, especially if for example your windscreen was cleaned while the vehicle is refuelled.

A road network of five, four and three-lane motorways serve Doha, which, despite the 120kmph speed limit, encourage speeding by being broad and relatively traffic free out of town. Fixed location and mobile speed radar with still and video cameras include sophisticated recognition systems including number plate; these allow the speedy imposition of fines. Vehicle number plates have the name Qatar in English and Arabic and only Hindu/Arabic numerals (the numbers used in the west). There is no regulation requiring any warning of a specific camera. Speed bumps and 'speed tables', with limited notice and visibility also attempt to slow traffic. If you hit one at speed, damage may occur to your chassis. Trucks are prohibited from using roads in Doha from 06:00 -08:00 / 12:00 - 15:00/ 17:00 - 22:00 due to the volume of traffic, you will find roads especially heavily congested during these hours.

For many short-term visitors, there will be a crucial couple of roads. Firstly Al Corniche which follows Doha Bay and gives immediate access to The National Museum, Museum of Islam Arts, Souq Waqif and West Bay. Al Corniche is a very scenic walk but at 7km is a walk for the cooler period of a day. It is also a direct route for public transport (bus route 76 & 777) connecting many of Qatar's principal tourist attractions.

The second key route is a driving route leading from Doha Port near the National Museum. This route is formed by the B Ring Rd, Al Khaleej St, Al Istiqlal St and Lusail Expressway that acts as an inner ring road skirting south of Souq Waqif and leading to Katara and The Pearl.

The original core of Doha focused on Souq Waqif, is now surrounded by a series of ring roads including the B Ring Rd. The inner one is now named Al Diwan St, then moving outward is B Ring Road, C, D, E (D & E combine to the west and become the Doha Expressway) F and G (which leads to the Salwa/Lusail Route. A less easily oriented series of roads form a network north and west of West Bay, with the north-south Lusail Expressway and west-east Onaiza St (which becomes Al Khafji St) being the key routes.

CAR HIRE

Qatar has numerous car hire companies including

Europcar   www.europcarqatar.com/;   Avis www.avisqatar.com/;Hertz   www.hertz.-com/rentacar/reservation/;And local including Al Mana (a two-hour   group)   http://www.almanaleasing.com/; Mustafawi   http://www.mustafawi.qa/;   Strong (http://www.strongrentacar.com/)   Rates   are   from QAR100/ per day.

If you use an international car-hire company, consider downloading their app that may make any booking a better experience.

To rent a car for up to seven days from several countries, including the EU / USA, your full driving licence should be acceptable, with suitable validity of vehicle type and period validity. For more than seven days, you will need an International driving licence or a license issued from a GCC (Gulf Cooperation Council) country. Also required will be your credit card with a minimum of 3 months validity; your passport will be photocopied, and fines will be payable before departure.

ACCIDENT REPORTING

To register a minor road accident, you can use Metrash2 app https://www.moi.gov.qa/site/english/metrash2/. You may obtain and activate Metrash 2 Service through SMS or Self Service Kiosk or helpdesk@moi.gov.qa you can use the following procedures: there must be a mobile number a registered in the applicant's name

Speak with the car hire company while receiving the vehicle regarding this app and accident regulations as requirements can change. In the event of an accident speak with the car hire company immediately to seek their updated advice as they may handle the below for you. Irrespective of the circumstances or blame remain calm and polite to other people involved.

In the event of injury

1/Phone 999 – Ambulance

2/Advise your location

3/Answer any questions from the emergency service

4/Follow their advice

For accidents, you can

1/ Supply no more than four pictures of each vehicle. One photograph should show the vehicles' number plates clearly.

2/ Move your vehicles from the scene and park away from the road.

3/ Ensure the location services of your phone are enabled.

4/ Sign in to Metrash2, select 'Traffic Services', open the 'Accident Report' option.

5/ Enter details of both vehicles (Vehicle No, driver identification number or driving licence, all resident of Qatar have an identification card, and mobile phone (cell phone) number – dial the other person's to ensure it is correct.)

6/ Attach photos of both vehicles and click on the agreement on the validity of the data.

7/ Submit the report for the traffic investigation police.

8/ A notification SMS (text message) will be sent to you asking to wait for another message to complete the procedures.

9/ After reviewing the accident photos by traffic investigators, an SMS will be sent to both parties with instructions to go to your insurance company for vehicle repair approval. The vehicle repair police report can be printed from the Ministry of Interior's official website, or through the insurance company concerned.

Taxi at Souq Waqif

TAXI

There are a variety of taxi services available, including Mowasalat car services. For their taxi bookings 800-TAXI (8294) +974 800 8294 (reduced mobility +9744458 8888 with advance notice 48hours+ ideal) , For limo reservations 800-LIMO (5466) (+974) 800 5466 , or download Karwa app (and ensure you have your exact location entered on map by GPS - if needed do it manually). Uber is available, as is Careem taxi (app available) a Gulf-wide taxi service offers a comparable service and fares to Uber.

In all app hailed taxi services the app is your payment system and cash, even if requested by the driver as might happen, is not a substitute and may lead to double payment or issues regarding your payment.

METRO

The Doha metro system will have three lines (Red, Gold, and Green) and 37 stations open by 2021 (more stations and an additional line may open after this). The Red Line, also known as the Coast Line, has three termini including **Hamad International Airport**. Two inter-changes, Al Bidda GPS 25.290608, 51.520262 and Msheireb GPS 25.282882, 51.526161 are within walking distance (max 1.2 km) to Souq Waqif. The line travels through West Bay and onto Lusail. The east-west Gold Line (Historic Line) stretches from Ras Bu Aboud to Al Aziziya. It includes the interchange at Msheireb and the stations at Souq Waqif GPS 25.287224, 51.534918 also for the Museum of Islamic Arts) and National Museum GPS 25.255575, 51.610805. The Green Line from Al Mansoura, in southern Doha, also passes through the two interchanges, Al Bidda and Msheireb and on west to Al Riffa.

A full day pass is available for QAR6/-.

From the airport bus station GPS 25.259276, 51.612450 Bus Route 109 serves Mesaieed to the south and Al Ghanim Bus Station GPS 25.285559, 51.536107 in central Doha. Route 777 travels along the Al Corniche to West Bay and 747 travels along Al Matar St into Al Ghanim Bus Station.

https://corp.qr.com.qa/English/Projects/Pages/Red Line.aspx

http://qatar.transit-guide.com/routes/

TRAM

A tram service is planned to operate from 2020 focused on Lusail town, with interchange options onto the metro Red Line at Lusail and Legtaifiya in the north of Doha.

BUS

A practical paid, shuttle coach services the general West Bay area runs every 15mins between 06:00-21:00. One 'circular' route travels from the General Post Office GPS 25.309565, 51.517023 via City Centre shopping Mall GPS 25.325920, 51.530500 and Doha Exhibition Centre GPS 25.322972, 51.527780, to the "W Hotel" GPS 25.328800, 51.529742 zig-zagging with several stops along the route. Friday is family only.

There are free shuttle bus services within the industrial area (west of Doha city centre) 88 will go between streets 1 (Salwa Road and Industrial Area) and street 52 (Abu Hamour Road and Industrial Area) and buses 16, 18, 61, and 81 will crisscross the area. These are principally targeted at workers in the industrial sector.

From Doha Al Ghanim Bus Station there are some longer distance national bus journeys, principally catering for immigrant labour and schoolchildren.

Route 100 from Doha Al Ghanim Bus Station to the north Madinat Al Shamal operates three times a day

09:30/15:30/21:30 - return 12:35/18:35/05:05 for the three hours innumerable stop journey. Route 101 is more frequent and is an hourly service from 04:10-19:10 and similar return timings. Routes 102/102X every half hour between 04:00-22:30 from Doha Al Ghanim Bus Station to Al Khor taking an hour and 10 minutes and from Al Khor route 201 for Madinat Al Shamal with a service every 90mins from 04:00-22:00 - and returns similar times.

Routes 104 & 104A travel from Doha Al Ghanim Bus Station west to Dukhan, every hour from 04:30-20:30 along with route 137 Three times a day at 13:30/17:30/21:30 and other direction from 08:36

There are a useful couple of services to Doha's south. One service, 109, serves Mesaieed (via the Airport) south of Doha every half hour from Doha Al Ghanim Bus Station starting from 04:09-23:09 with a half hour journey. One, route 136 travels south-west to Bu Samra (04:03-08:03-12:03-16:03-20:03 and similar returns for a two-hour trip).

These bus routes are less than QAR9, and the exact fare must be paid (no change is usually given) or with a KARWA smart-card (tap on boarding the bus and tap on exit). Buy the KARWA card at ticket vending machines at Hamad International Airport, Al Ghanim Bus Station, The Pearl Qatar and Qatar Mall and elsewhere. Cost QAR30 valid long term and can be topped up; QAR20 unlimited journeys in 24hours; QAR10 for two journeys in 24hours.

A private tourist service, The 'Doha Bus', offers a Hop on – Hop off type service (see tour operators below).

Less common as daily transport for western expats in Doha is using a bicycle. Carbon Wheels at The Pearl GPS 25.376059, 51.545497 12:00-21:00 (not Friday) offers products and repair service. Rides can be made at www.circuitlosail.com GPS 25.487484, 51.449094 +974 4472

9151 info@lcsc.qa. There are residents of Doha who cycle on the expressway road routes; however, for a visitor it would be prudent to ride with more locally experienced riders. There are some leisure cycling options in Aspire Park or Al Bidda Park

CHAPTER TWENTY-FOUR

MEDIA

Qatar, as an Arab country, is open to Arab language media from around the world, in much the same way as English language media from the USA is used in London and British media is used in New York.

Some of this 'pan-Arab' media is based within an Arab country, while others, especially if they have a critical approach to Arab governments, may be based in a non-Arab location, for example in London.

In Qatar, the relatively small population of Arab speakers required that local media received a subsidy through the government. This subsidy resulted in censorship, whether from the government or self-censorship. This support and overt government censorship was largely removed in 1995. Currently there are two Arabic papers Al Sharq, Al Watan.

English language papers include the Gulf Times www.gulf-times.com, The Peninsula www.thepeninsulaqatar.com and Qatar Tribune www.qatar-tribune.com. There are several Television stations including Taalam and

Baraaem, both aimed at children, Al Jazeera news and current affairs www.aljazeera.com/live/ also in Arabic and Arabic only Qatar Television (a government operation). Al Jazeera's news programs are claimed to be free of government political censorship, certainly it has replaced other channels as peoples preferred choice to source news.

There are a few magazines, including Expat Woman Qatar www.qatarexpatwomen.com, Time Out www.timeoutdoha.com.

Radio stations include Al Jazeera (Arabic and English) www.aljazeera.com/live/, Sout Al Khaleej (Arab and English www.soutalkhaleej.fm.

CHAPTER TWENTY-FIVE

Qatar has a single UNESCO World Heritage Site, **Al Zubarah**, a coastal town that is listed as "outstanding testimony to an urban trading and pearl-diving tradition which sustained the region's major coastal towns".

On the north-west coast of Qatar, Al Zubarah [p250] was a pearling and trading centre that flourished from around AD1760-1811. The town's establishment was probably a result of tribal migration from the town of Basra, Shatt Al Arab and the Kuwait area, a result of local conflicts. An initial settlement was probably established from AD1732 by people from the Al bin Ali family and the Al Khalifa family (currently rulers of Bahrain). These families are part of the large Utub tribal confederation, which includes the current day rulers of Bahrain and of Kuwait.

Al Zubarah fort

The plague hit Basra in the early AD1770s, which must have impacted its trade. Further migration from that area occurred during the Ottoman–Persian War of AD1775–1776. During the period that Al Zubarah was inhabited, there were several smaller settlements in northwest Qatar. Most seem to have been impacted by the rise and decline of Al Zubarah either negatively or positivity. The town follows the legacy of similar towns that developed around The Gulf, many of which traded with Mesopotamia in ancient times and then the Abbasid empire based in Baghdad. These small towns often served a small hinterland as well as trans-ocean trade.

Following an unsuccessful attack on Al Zubarah by the Persian governor of Bahrain in AD1783, Sheikh Ahmed bin Muhammad bin Khalifa invaded Bahrain from Al Zubarah and captured the island, which his descendants have ruled since. Al Zubarah was attacked from Riyadh by the Al Saud family forces from AD1787 and subsequently paid tribute to them. However the effect of the Al Saud occupation of the Al Ahsa oasis in Eastern Arabia increased the appeal of Al Zubarah, and many people fled into the town. In AD1809 Al Zubarah was occupied by the Al Saud. The Sultan of Oman (also called Imam of Oman) attacked the town in AD1811 during Egyptian attacks against the Al Saud in Riyadh with the result Al Zubarah was largely destroyed. This destruction created an opportunity for the Al Khalifa of Bahrain to reoccupy the town, though the occupants lived in a much smaller area.

From AD1868 the Al Khalifa were gradually excluded from the Qatar peninsula during a period of confrontations. The dispute between the Al Khalifa and the Al Thani family from Doha was complicated by the assertion of British power in The Gulf and decline of the Ottoman influence in the region, despite the Ottomans having several occupied forts and placed a governor located at Al Zubarah. Nonetheless, in AD1878 Sheikh Jassim bin Mohammed Al Thani captured the town, though subsequently, his hold was tenuous. Despite the town's decline, its proximity to Bahrain resulted in the building in 1938 of Al Zubarah Fort, following which Britain decided in 1939 that Al Zubarah was indeed part of sovereign Qatari territory. By 2001, ongoing territorial disputes between Bahrain and Qatar was finally settled by the International Court of Justice in The Hague, who adjudicated that Al Zubarah was Qatari territory, while at the same time Hawar Islands (off the Qatari west coast) were Bahraini territory.

©Vincent van Zeijst

Al Zubarah

The short period of Al Zubarah's occupation means that an authentic insight into the organisation of 18th & 19thc AD towns in the region can be gained. Windblown sand covered Al Zubarah, which concealed cemeteries, courtyard houses, walls, fishermen's huts, mosques, palaces, and narrow streets. Outside the town's walls are a canal and two screening walls, Al Zubarah Fort and another fort, Qalat Murair which is separated from Al Zubarah Fort by a road.

The town walls of Al Zubarah are the original outer wall and a smaller inner wall built after the town's AD1811 destruction. The outer wall is around 2500metres long, with 22 bastions at regular intervals. To the north, the wall extended west into the sea and formed part of a harbour. This wall, along with the town's overall grid-like layout, suggests a planned town layout. The smaller inner wall is built over previous structures and also made use of older building's material.

Two screening walls stretch out from the town towards Qalat Murair. These appear not only to defend the town generally but also offer immediate protection to people bringing water into town from water wells. In places, the walls run over a previous canal that may have provided access inland to boats and also helped supply water to the town.

The outer town wall enclosed up to 600 separate buildings, suggesting over 6,000people. Neighbourhoods in demarcated areas have been identified; again, most appear to have been planned. Most parts have the courtyard style housing that has been common throughout The Gulf; some seem to have had the iconic wind towers that are found throughout the region. Many of the buildings have gypsum decoration suggesting a degree of wealth enabling these decorative touches.

In the southern area of the town is a large fortified square palatial compound of just over one hectare with nine interior courtyards and a tower on each corner. Functions identified for some of its rooms include bathing areas and date processing rooms *madbasa* with the long troughs to collect date syrup that is pressed out from dates stored in sacks stacked on top of the channels.

A smaller compound to the north-east of the fortified square palatial compound has been partially excavated. This compound is just over half the size of the larger compound with towers on each corner. Both these compounds may have had an upper floor. One of two mosques so far identified is close to these two residential buildings. Early 20thcentury photos show it had substantial columns and arches supporting what is believed to be a multi-dome roof, all covered in plaster. Public squares are also found in this area of the town.

In the central area of the town, 80 metres east from the beach was a souq that not only engaged in import & export but also appears to have been involved in a range of processes including glass manufacture and the processing of dates for syrup. Close to it, on the beach, a small fort marked an area of deeper water to its south.

Huts that are believed to be associated with fishing and pearl diving have also been identified from postholes by the beach. Though here these are contemporary with Al Zubarah, this type of hut structure and its function remains prevalent throughout the region.

The town is on a ridge of slightly higher ground with the sea to its west and *sabkha* to the east. This landscape was established following the mid-Holocene period when the seawater levels in The Gulf were up to three metres above its current level. During this period, the sea was over a kilometre inland at Al Zubarah, after which it has retreated, stabilising around its current position about 1,500 years ago with *sabkha* replacing the sea.

The entire plain on which Al Zubarah is located without tree cover, testimony to the heat along with wind and lack of rain. Windblown sand and debris cover much of the entire town area, which is currently being excavated and therefore finds are continually being made.

Focused on Qalat Murair is a water canal, that stops about 500metres to its south-west. Though originally functional as a small boat canal, it appears to have been abandoned and partially infilled probably due to its functional or economic failure during Al Zubarah's existence.

Al Zubarah Fort was built by the ruler of Qatar, Sheikh Abdullah bin Jassim Al Thani in 1938 as a police outpost.

It was used as a military fort until the early 1970s. There is a photographic exhibition within the fort, about the old town of Al Zubarah. The construction followed a period of confrontation with Bahrain over the area and the Hawar Islands when a Bahraini police fort was built there in 1937. The single-story Al Zubarah Fort is of a type common throughout the Arabian Peninsula, with a large open court-yard within which is a water well and rooms opening off the courtyard.

Qalat Murair (Murair Fort – Qalat is the Arabic for fort) GSM 25.974456, 51.043402 was built in 1768 with a number out out-buildings along with water wells and a surrounding area of housing. Agriculture and livestock pens were to the fort's south and south-west. Its purpose appears to have been as a defence for the water canal. Today most of the remains are below the surface, and since it was occupied until the early 20th century, the stones may have been re-used for building the adjacent Al Zubarah Fort.

About 1,600metres north-east of Qalat Murair is a small fort Qalat Shuwail GSM 25.979637, 51.056855 that was noted in 1850 by Francis Warden Chief Secretary to the Government of India at Bombay. It is thought this fort is contemporary with Al Zubarah town.

Both Al Zubarah and Qalat Murair are on ground that is above the current *sabkha* and previous sea levels, shown by wave-cut platforms (levelled areas of rock or coral) offshore. The area around Qalat Murair is the location of the fresh water supply for Al Zubarah; this fresh water supply 'floats' over sea water intrusion into the land.

There are areas of scattered mangrove *Avicennia marina* along the shoreline and on the mud flats and the general inland areas salt tolerant plants close to Al Zubarah. In the sea occasional sightings of dugong *Dugong*

dugong and common bottlenose dolphin *Tursiops truncates* are made. Socotra cormorant *Phalacrocorax nigrogularis* are seen on Um Jatila Island just off Al Zubarah and greater flamingo *Phoenicopterus roseus* can be seen in winter, most easily close to the shore during high tide. Both green turtle *Chelonia mydas* and hawksbill turtle *Eretmochelys imbricata* have been seen in the water.

Some agriculture associated with Al Zubarah was developed 5km south-east of the town and at Al Jumail 18km north on the coast.

Under the Law of Antiquities of Qatar, it is a criminal offence to: excavate or remove any antiquities without permission from Qatar Museums or deface or otherwise damage any parts of a historical site.

Qatar also has three UNESCO inscriptions on the Representative List of the Intangible Cultural Heritage of Humanity.

Falconry as a sport is included in a UNESCO inscription. Falconry in Arabia is an ancient hunting practice mention by the Prophet Mohammed. The building between AD680-83, of falconry hunting lodges by Umayyad caliphs in the deserts of Syria and Jordan, is a testimony to the sport's prestige. Treaties on falconry were written, with peregrine *Falco peregrinus* and saker falcons *Falco cherrug* appearing to be the favoured birds and these continue to be the most favoured today. The history of falconry in The Gulf is little known as it was not, until recently, a written practice. Classically three species were a quarry for falcon hunting: the houbara bustard *Chlamydotis macqueenii*, the stone curlew *Burhinus oedicnemus*, and the Arabian hare *Lepus capensis*. The introduction of guns from the 16thcAD reduced the pressure to hunt with falcons and reduced the wildlife generally.

Falcons Souq Waqif

Today falconry is no longer what it must have been for originally, which was to obtain food and is a sport. Wild falcons are trapped during migration between September-November and then trained over the following weeks. In Qatar, captive falcons can be seen in Souq Waqif or near the Sealine Hotel south of Doha. There are various pieces of equipment associated with Falconry in The Gulf, the *burqa* (head hood) used to keep the bird calm; a *wakar* which is the stand on which the bird sits, *subuq* the tethers attached to the ankles, and of course a glove for the man called a *dass*, *kaff* or the more modern *mangaleh*. World Falconry Day is celebrated annually on 16th November, and Qatar holds a falconry festival, the Marmi Challenge, annually in January which exhibits falcons, saluki hunting dogs and hunting demonstrations.

Arabic Coffee as a demonstration of generosity and hospitality is included in this Intangible Cultural Heritage of Humanity list. The coffee uses green coffee beans, historically from Yemen. The process of preparing the coffee was traditionally done in front of guests. The beans are roasted lightly over a fire, pounded with a metal pestle and put in large copper coffee pot *dallah al logmah* with water and boiled. To add to the flavour, cardamom, cloves or other spices are added. After the coffee has brewed, it is poured into a small coffee pot *dallah al manzal*, from which it is poured into small cups *finjan*, that look like large thimbles. Usually, the most honoured guest is served first. Arabic coffee is often accompanied by dates, which are eaten first. When you have had enough coffee, after two or three cups is polite, return the cup to the person who serves you with a slight shake of the cup in your hand to signify, enough.

The third of these UNESCO inclusions is the system of holding a ***Majlis***, a meeting of people while sitting. A *majlis* is a formal space, either as a specific room in a building or, in *bedouin* society, it may have been outside. It forms a number of functions including a reception for outside guests, a celebration meeting or as a discussion area. Today a *majlis* is either a physical space, within a home or public building or is used a term to indicate a personal meeting between a number of people. In traditional society, a *majlis* is a single-sex meeting.

Arabic coffee serving and the *majlis* can be very formal occasions with guests assigned an often unobtrusive but noted hierarchy.

CHAPTER TWENTY-SIX

MAPS

These simple maps are a rough guidance, however you will find more detailed maps available in Qatar, if needed. Public transport is indicated within the locations text, with the appropriate station from the three metro lines. They are not intended to and do not indicate international borders, nor to they carry any authority regarding places names, their official spelling or precise location.

The GPS for each location is given, along with a street and area location. We think that the GPS will be most useful with a smart phone app, however as with all locational services they are only an indication and should be used with caution and in conjunction with an official map.

QATAR LOCATIONS

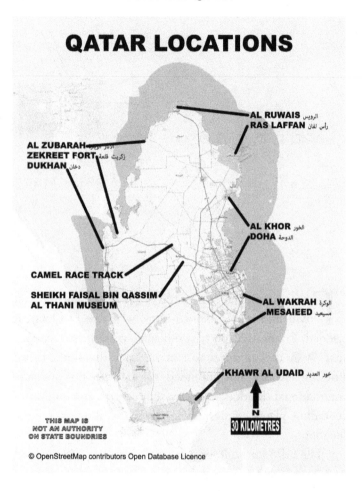

AL RUWAIS الرويس
RAS LAFFAN راس لفان

AL ZUBARAH الاثار الزبارة
ZEKREET FORT زكريت قلعة
DUKHAN دخان

AL KHOR الخور
DOHA الدوحة

CAMEL RACE TRACK

SHEIKH FAISAL BIN QASSIM
AL THANI MUSEUM

AL WAKRAH الوكرة
MESAIEED مسيعيد

KHAWR AL UDAID خور العديد

N

30 KILOMETRES

THIS MAP IS
NOT AN AUTHORITY
ON STATE BOUNDRIES

© OpenStreetMap contributors Open Database Licence

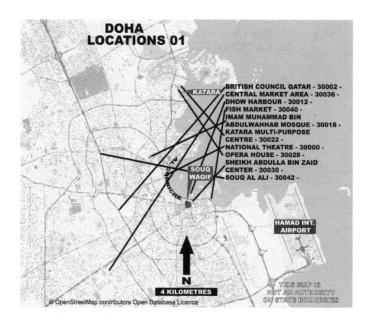

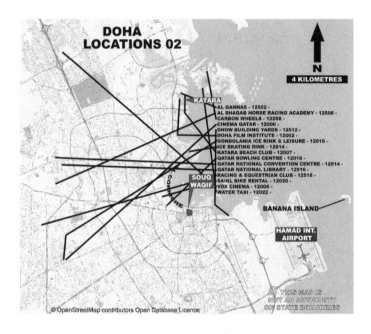

DOHA
LOCATIONS 02

N

4 KILOMETRES

KATARA

AL GANNAS - 12502 -
AL SHAQAB HORSE RACING ACADEMY - 12506 -
CARBON WHEELS - 12008 -
CINEMA QATAR - 12000 -
DHOW BUILDING YARDS - 12512 -
DOHA FILM INSTITUTE - 12002 -
GONDOLANIA ICE RINK & LEISURE - 12010 -
ICE SKATING RINK - 12014 -
KATARA BEACH CLUB - 12007 -
QATAR BOWLING CENTRE - 12016 -
QATAR NATIONAL CONVENTION CENTRE - 12514 -
QATAR NATIONAL LIBRARY - 12516 -
RACING & EQUESTRIAN CLUB - 12518 -
SAIKL BIKE RENTAL - 12020 -
VOX CINEMA - 12006 -
WATER TAXI - 12022 -

SOUQ
WAQIF

CORNICHE

BANANA ISLAND

HAMAD INT.
AIRPORT

THIS MAP IS
NOT AN AUTHORITY
ON STATE BOUNDARIES

© OpenStreetMap contributors Open Database Licence

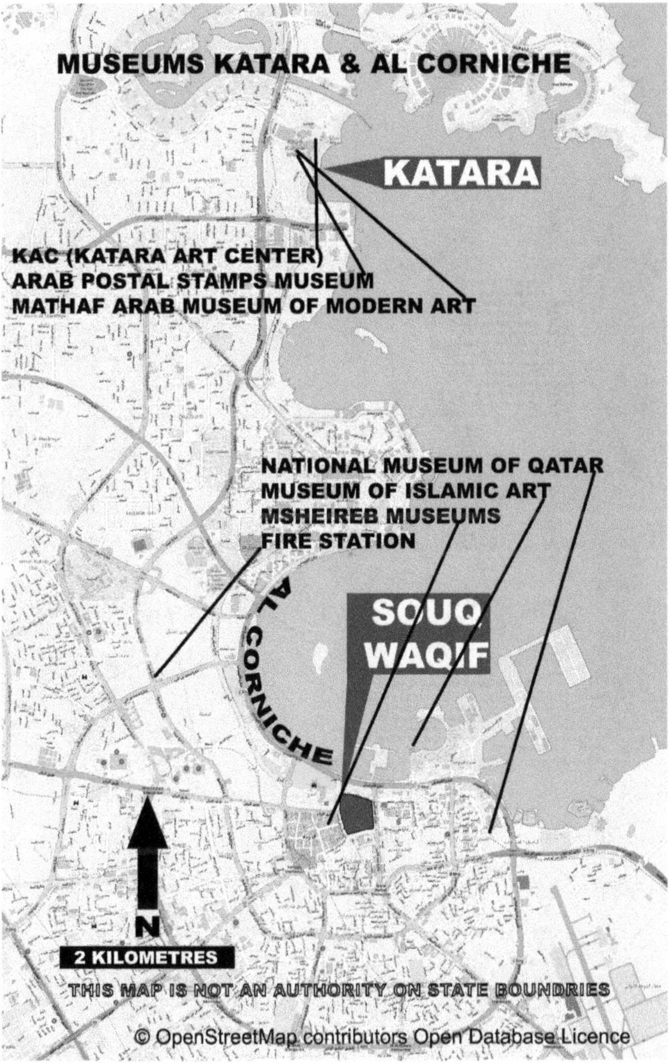

MUSEUMS KATARA & AL CORNICHE

KATARA

KAC (KATARA ART CENTER)
ARAB POSTAL STAMPS MUSEUM
MATHAF ARAB MUSEUM OF MODERN ART

NATIONAL MUSEUM OF QATAR
MUSEUM OF ISLAMIC ART
MSHEIREB MUSEUMS
FIRE STATION

AL CORNICHE

SOUQ WAQIF

N

2 KILOMETRES

THIS MAP IS NOT AN AUTHORITY ON STATE BOUNDARIES

© OpenStreetMap contributors Open Database Licence

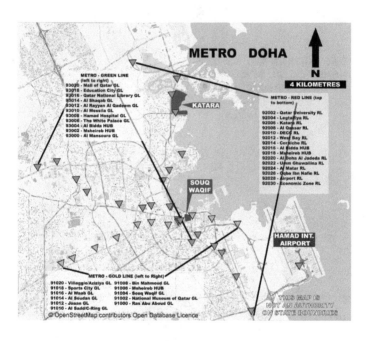

METRO DOHA

N

4 KILOMETRES

METRO - GREEN LINE
(left to right)
93020 - Mall of Qatar GL
93018 - Education City GL
93016 - Qatar National Library GL
93014 - Al Shaqab GL
93012 - Al Rayyan Al Qadeem GL
93010 - Al Messila GL
93008 - Hamad Hospital GL
93006 - The White Palace GL
93004 - Al Bidda HUB
93002 - Msheireb HUB
93000 - Al Mansoura GL

KATARA

METRO - RED LINE (top to bottom)
92002 - Qatar University RL
92004 - Legtaifiya RL
92006 - Katara RL
92008 - Al Qassar RL
92010 - DECC RL
92012 - West Bay RL
92014 - Corniche RL
92016 - Al Bidda HUB
92018 - Msheireb HUB
92020 - Al Doha Al Jadeda RL
92022 - Umm Ghuwailina RL
92024 - Al Matar RL
92026 - Qaba Ibn Nafie RL
92028 - Airport RL
92030 - Economic Zone RL

SOUQ WAQIF

HAMAD INT. AIRPORT

THIS MAP IS NOT AN AUTHORITY ON STATE BOUNDRIES

METRO - GOLD LINE (left to Right)
91020 - Villaggio/Aziziya GL   91008 - Bin Mahmoud GL
91018 - Sports City GL   91006 - Msheireb HUB
91016 - Al Waab GL   91004 - Souq Waqif GL
91014 - Al Soudan GL   91002 - National Museum of Qatar GL
91012 - Jòaan GL   91000 - Ras Abu Aboud GL
91010 - Al Sadd/C-Ring GL

© OpenStreetMap contributors Open Database Licence

CHAPTER TWENTY-SEVEN

EASY ITINERARIES

Cultural half day in Doha

Start with a visit to the impressive Museum of Islamic Arts [p148]. This visually imposing building is placed on a man-made island and overlooks the harbour in Doha. The building is set in a park and accessed by an avenue of date palms. The five floors hold an impressive collection of, as it says, Islamic Art.

Al Corniche

From the museum, take a 1.5-kilometer walk along Al Corniche into Souq Waqif [p153]. This souq was the original trading hub of Doha and today is a labyrinth of small shops, cultural sites and restaurants [p165] ranging from budget to luxuriously expensive, where you can refuel after your walk.

Museum full day in Doha

If you have a full day free in Doha, and want to immerse yourself in history and culture, this is for you.

The National Museum [p146] is an ideal place to begin. This was opened in 2019 and its focus is in general on the history and culture of Qatar. The design is based on the crystal 'desert rose' formation, though it could be also likened to a jumble of flying saucers.

Walk, or call a taxi, for the 2kilometer journey to the Museum of Islamic Arts [p148]. The walk will take you past the fish market. This museum is spread over five floors, with especially collected exhibits, the museum includes various temporary exhibitions and dining options.

Stroll along the Al Corniche for lunch in Souq Waqif [p153], where a great choice of options is listed [p165]. After lunch, Souq Waqif is an intriguing maze of shops and sights, including the falcon souq.

From Souq Waqif it's a short walk of 800metres to the Msheireb Museum's complex [p160]. These four buildings offer in insight into the cultural and social changes seen in Doha, over recent history.

Dune bashing and later a stroll through Katara full day.

South of Doha are the dunes bordering The Gulf. To experience this make a booking with your choice of tour operator. The drive from Doha is initially along expressways, before arriving into the powder like white dunes that spread like a carelessly tossed blanket. Check with your choice of **tour operator [p247]** about any lunch options by the sea.

Dunes and sea

Returning to Doha, organise that you are taken to Katara [p205]. Here within a distance of only 500metres is the Postal Stamp Museum [p205], a centre devoted to falcons and hunting [p209], restaurants [p213] and a plethora of sights.

CHAPTER TWENTY-EIGHT

LOCATIONS, RESTAURANTS, HOTELS

H otels Dollars
$0-60 *
$61-90 **
$91-125 ***
$126-190 ****
$191-250 *****
$251+ ******
Restaurants Dollars
$0-5 *
$5-9 **
$9-13 ***
$13-19 ****
$19-25 *****
$25 + ******

These are the lowest typical meal (excluding alcohol) price per person in a restaurant and lowest room price in a hotel. Add tipping as appropriate.

Overall the included hotels and restaurants offer a choice to consider within their price range.

Major hotels, and the restaurants within them, will usually have alcohol available; Ramadhan may affect its availability.

In general brand name 'international' hotels do offer the most consistent service. In the lower price range, especially hotels that are not part of an international group, service may be patchy and in these hotels that are more than a few years old, lack of maintenance starts to impact their quality.

All hotels and restaurants rely on staff who work on a contract of a couple of years within Qatar. This means that the constant change in staff will affect how well they can manage their business which may result in changes of service levels and overall quality.

Areas below are subjective simply to make groupings of places easier. In each area attractions that a visitor may find interesting are included along with hotels and restaurants. The GPS location is given, along with a street and area location. We think that the GPS will be most useful. The simple maps above are a rough guidance, however you will find more detailed maps available in Qatar, if needed. Public transport is indicated, with the appropriate station from the three metro lines.

A L CORNICHE, SOUQ WAQIF & CENTRAL DOHA

AL CORNICHE الكورنيش -: *Type of Location* PUBLIC PLACE -: **GPS** 25.291421, 51.533743 -: *Street* - Al Corniche -: *Public Transport if available* - Bus 76, 777 (Airport), Metro Gold Line Souq Waqif -: *Town / Area* - Souq Waqif سوق واقف -: *Opening Hours* - 24 Hours -

: ***Entrance & cost*** No charge -: *Description* - The sweep of Al Corniche takes you past the National Museum Qatar, Museum of Islamic Arts, Dhows, Souq Waqif, Park and towards the almost psychedelic illuminations of West Bay at night. There are numerous stops on the walk of around seven kilometres so allow a couple of hours, if you like diversions add more time; the best time is late afternoon to enjoy the sunset and lights coming on in West Bay. Cut into Souq Waqif & Al Bidda Park for a change of scenery. A bottle of water in hand is ideal, along with your camera. There are limited crossing options – Al Meena St offers one opportunity between National and Islamic Arts museums and one adjacent to The Pearl monument can give access into Souq Waqif-: *Book reference number* 12624

DHOW BUILDING YARDS مصنع السفن -: *Type of Location* LEISURE CULTURE -: ***GPS*** 25.284646, 51.560431 -: *Street* - Ras Al Aboud Expressway -: *Public Transport if available* - Bus 109,777 Metro GoldLine National Museum -: *Town / Area* - Al Corniche الكورنيش -: *Opening Hours* - appx 08:00-17:00 -: ***Entrance & cost*** No Charge -: *Phone* - -: *Email* - -: *Description* - Easily reached on the eastern part of the Al Corniche is a small Dhow Building Yard. This is a private operation, however a smile and a request to look is usually answered with a 'welcome'. Unfortunately, this is prime real estate and sooner rather than later may disappear. Worth dropping in if you visit the Islamic or National Museums. -: *Book reference number* 12512

NATIONAL MUSEUM OF QATAR متحف قطر الوطني -: *Type of Location* MUSEUM -: ***GPS*** 25.286512, 51.548038 -: *Street* - On Museum Park St near the east Al

Corniche extension -: *Public Transport if available* - Bus 76, 109 Metro Gold Line National Museum -: *Town / Area* - Al Corniche الكورنيش -: *Opening Hours* - Sun-Wed 09:00 to 19:00 / Thurs 09:00 to 21:00 / Fri from 11:30 to 21:00 / Sat 09:00 to 21:00 -: **Entrance & cost** QAR50 / all Qatar Museum's pass (this is the organisation's name not a general pass to all museums this pass includes Museum of Islamic Art, Mathaf and National Museum of Qatar – visit 3 for the price of 2) QAR100 – tickets have a validity of three consecutive days from the date of initial admission - concessions for children and Qatar's residents -: *Email* – infonmoq@qm.org.qa -: *WebSite* - www.nmoq.org.qa -:

National Museum Qatar

Description - National Museum Qatar's ground work started in 2012 in the area around the original Palace of Sheikh Abdullah bin Jassim Al-Thani which was built in 1901 and occupied by Sheikh Abdullah and his sons until 1933. The design by Jean Nouvel was inspired by the crystal formations of gypsum found in sandy deserts called 'Desert Rose' because of their clustered petal-like appearance. Inside the museum, its walls all seem to be sloping out of the vertical creating a non-conventional backdrop for exhibits. The collections highlight Qatar from pre-history to its modern. Exhibits include Qatar's flora, fauna, and cultural display, with modern multi-media to enhance physical objects. There is some overlap or spill over of exhibits that might fit into the Museum of Islamic Arts.

National Museum Qatar

The concept is to show a connection with Qatar's history by the relationship between the old Palace and the new Museum. A must see. -: *Book reference number* 12610

FISH MARKET سوق السمك -: *Type of Location* TOURIST SOUQ -: *GPS* 25.2913572, 51.547537 -: *Street* - Al Corniche (east) -: *Public Transport if available* - Bus 76, 109 Metro Gold Line National Museum -: *Town / Area* - Al Corniche الكورنيش -: *Opening Hours* - best in morning 24 Hours -: *Entrance & cost* No Charge -: *Description* - A small market for fresh fish, with fish unloaded directly off the small boats. The best time is early morning -: *Book reference number* 30040

MUSEUM OF ISLAMIC ART متحف الفن الإسلامي -: *Type of Location* MUSEUM -: *GPS* 25.294570, 51.539300 -: *Street* - Eastern end of Al Corniche -: *Public Transport if available* - Bus 76, 777 Metro Gold Line Souq Waqif -: *Town / Area* - Al Corniche الكورنيش -: *Opening Hours* - Sat-Thurs 09:00-19:00 Fri 13:30:19:00 -: *Entrance & cost* QAR50 / all Qatar Museum's pass QAR100 (the organisation not a general pass to all Museums in Qatar this includes the Museum of Islamic Art, Mathaf and National Museum of Qatar – visit 3 for the price of 2) – tickets have a validity of three consecutive days from the date of initial admission - concessions for children and Qatar's residents -: *Phone* - +974 4422 4444 -: *Email* – contact form -: *WebSite* - www.mia.org.qa -:

Museum of Islamic Art

Description - The Museum of Islamic Art is a significant centre for the collection, display and study of Islamic art from around the world. The museum, which opened in 2008, is a five-story, purpose-built building on a man-made island with a geometric exterior design and spacious interior. A public park surrounds it to the general area to the south, east and north, while the dhow harbour is to the west. Most of the collection was specifically purchased for the museum, and the size of the halls enable each piece to be superbly displayed. In addition to the permanent collection, there are regular temporary exhibitions.

A library opens with similar opening hours though it is closed Friday. The prestige of this museum does make it a must see - however, although the individual pieces are of world-class quality, the collection is less numerous than other comparable institutions. The National Museum and Souq Waqif make ideal additions to a visit -: *Book reference number* 12608

AL RIWAQ GALLERY

Museum of Islamic Arts

-: **معرض ، الرواق** : *Type of Location* GALLERY -: **GPS** 25.293564, 51.543248 -: *Street* – east of drive to Museum of Islamic Arts -: *Public Transport if available* - Bus 76, 777 Metro Gold Line Souq Waqif -: *Town / Area* - Al Corniche **الكورنيش** -: *Opening Hours* – 09:00-18:30 -:

Entrance & cost QAR50 / all Qatar Museum's (the organisation not a general pass this includes Museum of Islamic Art (and Al Riwaq), Mathaf and National Museum of Qatar – visit 3 for the price of 2) QAR100 – tickets have a validity of three consecutive days from the date of initial admission - concessions for children and Qatar's residents -: *Phone* - +974 4422 4444 -: *Email* – contact form -: *WebSite* - www.mia.org.qa -: *Description* – small art exhibition space with changeable displays. A very short walk from the Museum of Islamic Arts.

7 (Seven) -: *Type of Location* SCULPTURE -: **GPS** 25.298012, 51.539693 -: *Street* - Museum of Islamic Art -: *Public Transport if available* - Bus 76, 777 Metro Gold Line Souq Waqif -: *Town / Area* - Al Corniche **الكورنيش** -: *Opening Hours* - 24 Hours -: *Description* - 7 by Richard Serra represents the multiplicity of meanings the number 7 has in Islam. It also makes a fitting terminus to the park behind the Islamic Museum and an ideal location to watch the skyscrapers light up at dusk. -: *Book reference number* 15000

DHOW HARBOUR ميناء الداو -: *Type of Location* LEISURE LOCATION -: *GPS* 25.294827, 51.534615 -: *Street* - Off Al Corniche near Souq Waqif -: *Public Transport if available* - Bus 76, 777 Metro Gold Line Souq Waqif -: *Town / Area* - Al Corniche الكورنيش -: *Opening Hours* - 24 Hours -: *Description* - Here are a multiplicity of Dhows, anchored off the jetty along with modern boats. Sea excursions leave from the dock including from the Anantara reception to the Banana Resort Island, there is a small car park (parking lot) if needed. The general jetty (here called a harbour) offers an excellent opportunity to see Dhows close up as well as get a different angle for photographs of Doha. As part of an afternoon walk or a photographic trip, this is worth stopping off at. The small island in the centre of the harbour was, until 2006, a small resort hotel; it must be waiting for a new development, possibly a water fountain. -: *Book reference number* 30012

Pearl Monument

THE PEARL MONUMENT اللؤلؤة -: *Type of Location* SCULPTURE -: ***GPS*** 25.291421, 51.533743 -: *Street* - Al Corniche -: *Public Transport if available* - Bus 76, 777 (Airport), Metro Gold Line Souq Waqif -: *Town / Area* - Souq Waqif سوق واقف -: *Opening Hours* - 24 Hours -: *Description* - This is in the shape of an open Oyster with a Pearl inside, with a water cascade that empties into the sea. It's a useful 'place mark' along with the helical minaret on the Islamic Cultural Centre. -: *Book reference number* 15022

ISLAMIC CULTURAL CENTRE (SHEIKH ABDULLA BIN ZAID AL MAHMOUD) مركز الشيخ عبد الله بن زيد ال محمود الثقافي الإسلامي -: *Type of Location* LEISURE LOCATION -: ***GPS*** 25.288877, 51.536134 -: *Street* - Junction Abdulla bin Jassim St and Hamid Al Kabir

St - east of Souq Waqif. -: *Public Transport if available* - Bus 76, 177 Metro Gold Line Souq Waqif -: *Town / Area* - Souq Waqif سوق واقف -: *Opening Hours* - 05:00-20:00 -: **Entrance & cost** No Charge -: *Phone* - 44447444 -: *Email* - binzaid@islam.gov.qa -: *WebSite* - www.binzaid.-gov.qa -: *Description* - This centre, also called Al Fanar, explains and promotes Islam and Qatar's culture. Inside are prayer rooms and lecture halls. Arabic language lessons are offered. The centre is useful if you wish authoritative information about Islam in Qatar. The helical minaret of the building is a useful prominent landmark. It takes its design from the Malwiya minaret of Great Mosque in Samarra Iraq. -: *Book reference number* 30030

SOUQ WAQIF سوق واقف -: *Type of Location* TOURIST SOUQ -: **GPS** 25.289410, 51.533581 -: *Street* - Junction Abdullah bin Jassim St and Hamid Al Kabir St - south of Pearl Monument on Al Corniche St and jetty for Dhows. The Gold Line Souq Waqif Station and Msheireb Central Metro (Hub) are within 350m and 800m respectfully. -: *Public Transport if available* - Bus 76, 177 Metro Gold Line Souq Waqif -: *Town / Area* - Souq Waqif سوق واقف -: *Opening Hours* - The souq is made up of individual businesses with their own hours. Most shops open between 10:00-12:00/16:00-22:00 and restaurants from 10:00-22:00 - Ramadhan timings will vary. -: **Entrance & cost** No charge to enjoy the atmosphere. -:

Horsemen Souq Waqif

Description - Souq Waqif is probably the most visited tourist attraction in Doha. As with many souqs in coastal Arabia, Souq Waqif (which means the standing market) was set up close to the sea, where boats could unload their goods, on either side of a wadi (Wadi Msheireb), which in dry weather provided an open space for people to walk between stalls, the standing was because of its lack of sitting places. In origin, the date for the souq must be similar to the origin date for Doha, which grew from the AD1820s.

The Ottomans became established as a power from AD1871, and Al Koot Fort (on the west of Souq Waqif) was built in AD1880, which must have increased trade for the merchants. In 1927 the Amir of Qatar rebuilt the fort, establishing this area as the centre of Doha. New shopping areas after the oil and gas boom resulted in the loss of trade and a catastrophic fire destroyed many businesses. The government started restoration to a pre-1950 state. Traditional construction materials such as mangrove tree poles and date palm matting are combined with modern air-conditioning to create what many feel is one of the best traditional souqs in Arabia.

Souq Waqif

The range of outlets includes shopping, restaurants (see below) and cultural attractions. The change in the economy in Qatar towards modern shopping malls resulted in a decline in Souq Waqif that was compounded by a major fire in 2003. The entire area was either rebuilt or renovated to create a style of the souq from before 1950. There is substantial underground car parking (parking lot) , excellent transport links and several boutique hotels which as well as being a leading tourist attraction creates a base for any visit to Doha.

Numerous places to eat line the streets, with covered shopping areas behind the main pedestrian area (see restaurants). To the west is the **camel pen** area off Al Jasra St

GPS 25.289651, 51.531727 **Falcon Souq GPS** 25.288701, 51.530632 between Al Jasra St & Al Asmakh St and temporary **stabling for horses GPS** 25.289105, 51.530384 off Al Asmakh St.

Falcon and owner in Souq Waqif

The Falcon Souq opens roughly 09:00-12:30 /17:00-21:00 (Fridays only in the afternoon). The best time to visit is in the afternoon, ideally Thursday, when potential buyers visit to check out the birds. Just to the north of this is the Falcon Hospital, it's interesting though not normally open for casual visits.

GOLD AND CRAFT SOUQS -: *Type of Location*

SHOPPING -: *GPS* 25.287114, 51.533383 -: *Street –* Souq Waqif St / Al Ahmed St. The Gold Line Souq Waqif Station and MSHEIREB CENTRAL METRO STATION are within 350m and 800m respectfully. -: *Public Transport if available* - Bus 76, 177 Metro Gold Line Souq Waqif -: *Town / Area* - Souq Waqif سوق واقف -: *Opening Hours* – 09:00-12:00 / 15:00-21:00 Sat-Fri -: *Description* – Gifts and gold in a colourful setting. The gold is ornate Gulf style at 19 carat plus, if you search you may find simpler designs. Prices can be negotiated down by 5-10%. If its handicraft bargain more. -: *Book reference number* 30033

POLICE & TOURIST SUPPORT -: *Type of Location* LEISURE LOCATION -: *GPS* 25.286926, 51.533037 -: *Street –* Souq Waqif St. The Gold Line Souq Waqif Station and MSHEIREB CENTRAL METRO STATION are within 350m and 800m respectfully. -: *Public Transport if available* - Bus 76, 177 Metro Gold Line Souq Waqif -: *Town / Area* - Souq Waqif سوق واقف -: *Opening Hours* – 09:00-12:00 / 15:00-18:00 Sun-Thurs -: *Phone* – Call Centre +974 4406 9921 -: *WebSite* - www.visitqatar.qa *Description* - An ideal stop for tourist information in Souq Waqif -: *Book reference number* 30032

The core of the souq is less than three hectares while the larger area is under twenty hectares. To put this into context, the core area is comparable to the ground space of the Palace of Versailles and the larger area about 25% of only the ornamental gardens immediately next to Versailles. This does mean that as a location, it is comfortable to explore. If you only have time to visit one place in Doha, this is it. -: *Book reference number* 30044

WIND TOWER HOUSE بيت الملاقف -: *Type of*

Location HISTORICAL -: *GPS* 25.285442, 51.533480 -
: *Street* - Junction of Grand Hamid St (Banks St) and Ali
bin Abdullah St - inside the courtyard of Souq Al Najada
-: *Public Transport if available* - Bus - Al Ghanim Bus
Station Metro Red/Gold/Green Lines Interchange
Msheireb -: *Town / Area* - Msheireb مشيرب -: *Opening
Hours* - not open. *Description* - An authentic Wind
Tower House set in an incongruous location within the
rebuilt Souq Al Najada. Wind towers are usually four-
sided towers that are part of a building, usually a house
and rise substantially above it. The upper part of the
tower is open on each side and roofed. A wall within the
tower directs the wind down to provide a breeze into the
house. Water evaporators at some place in the tower
might add to the cooling effect. This is currently not open
but previously was a museum. Worth passing by, if possible, on the way to Souq Waqif. -: *Book reference number*
10022

Al Koot Fort

AL KOOT FORT قلعة الكوت -: Type of Location
HISTORICAL -: GPS 25.286851, 51.530886 -: Street -
south of Souq Waqif -: Public Transport if available - Bus -
Al Ghanim Bus Station Metro Red/Gold/Green Lines
Interchange Msheireb -: Town / Area - Souq Waqif سوق

واقف -: Opening Hours - 08:00-12:00 (opening does seem to be at random) -: Entrance & cost No charge -: Description - Just to the south-west of Souq Waqif near the underground carpark entrance is Al Koot Fort. Built in 1880 during the Turkish period, its presence must have increased trade for the merchants. In 1927, the Amir of Qatar rebuilt the fort establishing this area as the centre of Doha. This secured Souq Waqif, shipping and camel trains supplying the souq and boats. Inside has been an exhibition of handicrafts; however, currently there are no displays. The opening of the fort is at random so do ask if you see an open gate. This fort is very easy to get to and makes a good addition to a visit to Souq Waqif -: Book reference number 10004

Msheireb Museum Company House

MSHEIREB MUSEUMS متاحف مشيرب -: *Type of Location* MUSEUM -: *GPS* 25.287093, 51.529370 -: *Street* - East side of Al Asmakh St -: *Public Transport if available* - Bus 76, 177 Metro Msheireb (Hub) -: *Town / Area* - Msheireb مشيرب -: *Opening Hours* - Sunday: Closed Monday to Thursday: 09:00 – 17:00 Friday: 15:00pm – 21:00 Saturday: 09:00 –17:00 -: ***Entrance & cost*** No Charge -: *Phone* - +974 40065555 -: *Email* - museums@msheireb.com -: *WebSite* - www.msheireb.com -: *Description* - Msheireb Museums is four 'houses' each with a different past and theme. The museum is a fusion of traditional and modern to illustrate the modern history of Doha. 'Company House' Set within a house that was once used as the headquarters for Qatar's first oil company, this museum tells the story of the pioneering Qatari petroleum industry workers and their families, who helped transform Qatar into a modern society. The 'Bin Jelmood House' provides space for reflection on the story of slavery and its trade in Qatar and the broader Gulf, which still is little acknowledged within the region, and how it has evolved into modern forms of human exploitation. Unique in The Gulf region, unusual in the world it is a concept for a museum that many capital cities lack. Bin Jelmood House also provides an opportunity for visitors to make a personal commitment to joining the fight against human exploitation in all its many manifestations. Radwani House provides visitors with an insight into how family life evolved in Qatar over the years. The house showcases not only how Qatar changed over time, but also how domestic family life was transformed in Doha. On the other side of the road (next to Msheireb Mosque) is Mohammed bin Jassim House Built by Sheikh Mohammed Bin Jassim Al-Thani, son of the founder of modern Qatar, this heritage house addresses the past, the present and the sustainable aspect on which Msheireb Downtown Doha is based. Well worth a visit this is a well laid out collection and very easy to get to from Souq Waqif, across Al Asmakh St, past the Falcon Souq. -: *Book reference number* 12606

AL BIDDA, AL RUMAILA, WADI AL SAIL PARKS 'DOHA GRAND PARK' الحدائق البدع و الرميلة و وادي السيل -: *Type of Location* PUBLIC PLACE -: *GPS* 25.298460, 51.515600 -: *Street* - West of the Al Corniche -: *Public Transport if available* - Bus 100, 101,102,102X,170,172 , Metro Red Line/Green Line Al Bidda -: *Town / Area* - Al Bidda park area حديقة البدع -: *Opening Hours* - 24 Hours -: ***Entrance & cost*** No charge -: *Description* - Al Bidda Park is a substantial land-scaped park on the Al Corniche in central Doha. The total area is around 1.7 sq km (slightly larger than Hyde Park London) and includes a water feature, cafes, a children's park 25.303143, 51.514019 and maze. There are designated sports areas including for tennis, cycle paths and outdoor gym. Specific barbeque areas need to be used for cooking while there are several small cafes spread over the park. Toilets and first aid is available. Walkways give access over roads from one area to the next. Underground car parks give access from Al Corniche (southbound) and Uhud St. Busiest at the weekend and after 16:00hrs. Probably not a critical part of a visit to Doha, it does add a relaxing part to any visit and certainly is in a fantastic location next to the sea and with skyscrapers in the distance, if walking along the Al Corniche, take a diversion through the park. -: *Book reference number* 12622

SAIKL BIKE RENTAL -: *Type of Location* LEISURE ACTIVITY -: *GPS* 25.298365, 51.512893 -:

Street - Off Al Khaleej St / Al Bidda Park -: *Public Transport if available* - Bus 100, 101,102,102X,170,172 , Metro Red Line/Green Line Al Bidda -: *Town / Area* - Al Bidda park area حديقة البدع -: *Opening Hours* - 16:00-02:00 (after midnight) -: ***Entrance & cost*** from QAR20 for 30mins - with a variety of bikes for all the family -: *Phone* - +974 5028 0404 -: *Email* - info@saiklqtr.com -: *WebSite* - www.saiklqtr.com -: *Description* - Bikes rented for adults and children by the Hour (with helmets) also bike service -: *Book reference number* 12020

QATAR BOWLING CENTRE مركز قطر للبولينج -: *Type of Location* LEISURE ACTIVITY -: ***GPS*** 25.291930, 51.516164 -: *Street* - off Khaleej St / Al Bidda Park -: *Public Transport if available* - Bus 100, 101,102,102X,170,172 , Metro Red Line/Green Line Al Bidda -: *Town / Area* - Al Corniche الكورنيش -: *Opening Hours* - Sat-Wed 09:00-24:00 Thurs 09:00-02:00(night) Fri 09:00-01:00(night) -: ***Entrance & cost*** QAR 20 upwards -: *Phone* - +974 4432 9178 -: *Email* - qatarbowlingfederation@gmail.com -: *WebSite* - www.qatarbowlingfederation.com -: *Description* - With a World Champion Bowling Team - this is the bowling centre in Doha where they hold international events which may affect opening schedules. There are 32 lanes, Billiards and Table Tennis and Café. -: *Book reference number* 12016

FIRE STATION الدفاع المدني -: *Type of Location* MUSEUM -: ***GPS*** 25.302517, 51.507310 -: *Street* - junction Mohammed bin Thani St and Al Istiqlal St -: *Public Transport if available* - Bus 101,102, 102X, 170 Metro Red Line Corniche (1500metres) -: *Town / Area* - Al Bidda park area حديقة البدع -: *Opening Hours* - Sat-Thurs 09:00-21:00 -: ***Entrance & cost*** QAR50 non-residents of Qatar or all

Museum 3 day pass QAR100 -: *Phone* - +974 4422-4222 -: *Email* - contact@firestation.org.qa -: *WebSite* - www.firestation.org.qa -: *Description* - This at its heart is a small art incubator to develop artists from Qatar to develop their talent. A finishing exhibition is held. Rotating exhibits of other art are held. An artist's supply shop retails art material. There is a small theatre for public events, and a café #999 is open to relax in, next to Al Bidda Park. The Fire Station is comparable to Mathaf (below), and with its convenient location and park-like surroundings makes it a worthwhile stop for modern art lovers. -: *Book reference number* 12602

NATIONAL THEATRE المسرح الوطني -: *Type of Location* LEISURE LOCATION -: *GPS* 25.305291, 51.515746 -: *Street* - off Al Corniche -: *Public Transport if available* - Bus 76, 777 Metro Red Line Corniche -: *Town / Area* - Al Corniche الكورنيش -: *Opening Hours* - 07:00-14:00 Sun-Thurs / 16:45-21:15 -: *Entrance & cost* -: *Phone* - +974 4483 6118 -: *WebSite* - https://www.dohafilminstitute.com/venues/qatar-national-theatre -: *Description* - Pubic Arts venue for theatre plays, concerts and art cinema. There are several events each week. -: *Book reference number* 30000

IMAM MUHAMMAD BIN ABDULWAHHAB MOSQUE جامع الإمام مُحمَّد بن عبد الوهاب -: *Type of Location* LEISURE LOCATION -: *GPS* 25.317514, 51.506532 -: *Street* - Junction Khalifa St and Al Istiqlal St -: *Public Transport if available* - Bus 100,101,102,102x 170 -: *Town / Area* - Al Jebailat الجبيلات -: *Opening Hours* - Open to non-Muslims during non-prayer times. 08:00-11:30 / 14:00-15:00 / 17:00-18:00 / 21:00-22:00 Always check newspapers for each days prayer times. -: *Entrance &*

cost No Charge -: *Phone* - oo 974 4470 oooo -: *Email* -
binzaid@islam.gov.qa -: *WebSite* - www.binzaid.gov.qa -:
Description - This is the largest mosque in Doha and is
open to non-Muslims. It is preferable for non-Muslims to
visit outside prayer times, most especially midday prayers,
as you will then be able to move more easily. Though the
timings given here do allow for timing variations
throughout the year, do check the actual prayer times in
Doha on the day you wish to visit before you arrive.

Imam Muhammad ibn Abd al-Wahhab Mosque

Children under seven are not permitted. Commercial
photography is not permitted, sometimes photography is
only permitted using mobile-phone (cell phone) and all
photography is excluded in the ladies prayer rooms. Men
should wear long trousers and long-sleeved shirts, avoiding
text on them. Women should be wear clothing that only
shows face, hands and feet. The mosque issues headscarf
and abaya to wear if needed. Each sex can only visit the

appropriate area in the mosque. The mosque opened in 2011 and is named after the Islamic theologian (see religion chapter) from the 18thc AD who lived in Riyadh Saudi Arabia. In keeping with an austere version of Islam, the mosque is plainly decorated. Inside there are separate prayer rooms for men and women also several libraries, with some books in English. The floor space for the men's room is 7,400sqm, and the entire building has three floors. The 93 domes refer to the multi-dome mosques in Makkah and Al Madina. Guided tours available through the website www.binzaid.gov.qa or visit Islamic Cultural Centre (Sheikh Abdulla Bin Zaid Al Mahmoud Al Fanar). An ideal time to visit is before the prayers (around sunset) and then enjoy the panorama over the city as the skyscrapers are illuminated and the call to prayer is made. Call your Uber style taxi to leave the mosque as this is relatively isolated from main routes. To visit an Islamic country, especially for the first time and not visit a mosque is an omission. -: *Book reference number* 30018

RAS ABU ABBOUD -: *Type of Location* SPORT 2022 -: *GPS* 25.288917, 51.565114 -: *Street* - Ras Abu Abboud St -: *Public Transport if available* - Bus 109,777 Metro Gold Line National Museum -: *Town / Area* - Ras Abu Abboud راس أبو عبود -: *Opening Hours* - As per event -: *Description* - A stadium for the 2022 World Cup -: *Book reference number* 21018

Restaurants in Souq Waqif

SHUJAA RESTAURANT -: *Type of Location* RESTAURANT -: *GPS* 25.289341, 51.532951 -: *Street* - near Corniche in Souq Waqif -: *Public Transport if available* - Bus 76, 177 Metro Gold Line Souq Waqif -: *Town / Area* - Souq Waqif سوق واقف -: *Opening Hours* - 14:00-

oo:oo -: ***Cost per person appx*** * -: *Phone* - +974 5586
7895 -: *Email* - -: *Description* - Small, always busy and inexpensive, share your table with others. Meat-based dishes are
available in the evening. A stone's throw away from the
opulence of Parisa; it's hard to say which is more enjoyable.
-: *Book reference number* 14018

AL ADHAMIYAH IRAQI RESTAURANT -:

Type of Location RESTAURANT -: ***GPS*** 25.286300,
51.531745 -: *Street* - Ali Bin Abdullah St, Doha, Qatar -:
Public Transport if available - Bus Al Ghanim Bus Station
Metro Gold Line Souq Waqif -: *Town / Area* - Souq Waqif
سوق واقف -: *Opening Hours* - 12:30-00:00 (Midnight) -:
Cost per person appx ** -: *Phone* - +974 4432 4326 -:
Description - Very popular Iraqi meat & rice based restaurant. Outside or inside dining with great fruit juices. Slack
service reflects how busy they are and also relatively low
cost. -: *Book reference number* 14026

BANDAR ADEN -: *Type of Location* RESTAU-

RANT -: ***GPS*** 25.289576, 51.532839 -: *Street* - Abdullah
Bin Jassim St, -: *Public Transport if available* - Bus 76, 177
Metro Gold Line Souq Waqif -: *Town / Area* - Souq Waqif
سوق واقف -: *Opening Hours* - 06:00-23:00 (Friday 12:30-
23:00) -: ***Cost per person appx*** ** -: *Phone* - +974
44375503 -: *Email* - bandaraden@yahoo.com -: *WebSite* -
http://www.bandaraden.com/ -: *Description* - Authentic, in
all respects from food (meat and rice based), very patchy
service and poor cleanliness. Very popular, they must be
getting something right. Ask for cutlery. -: *Book reference
number* 14032

AL SHURFA ARABIC RESTAURANT -: *Type of*

Location RESTAURANT -: ***GPS*** 25.289395, 51.533223 -
: *Street* - off Al Corniche -: *Public Transport if available* -

Bus 76, 177 Metro Gold Line Souq Waqif -: *Town / Area* -
Souq Waqif سوق واقف -: *Opening Hours* - 12:00-00:00 -:
Cost per person appx *** -: *Phone* - +974 4433 6666 -:
Email - res.vswq@tivolihotels.com -: *WebSite* -
https://www.tivolihotels.com/en/souq-waqif-al-jomrok-
boutique-hotel? -: *Description* - One of the more interesting
views in Doha, coupled with the flavour of the Middle East
makes a good dinner choice. One of two restaurants within
the small Al Jumrok Hotel -: *Book reference number* 14048

THE VILLAGE -: *Type of Location* RESTAURANT
-: ***GPS*** 25.286909, 51.532748 -: *Street* - Al Souq St -:
Public Transport if available - Bus Al Ghanim Bus Station
Metro Gold Line Souq Waqif -: *Town / Area* - Souq Waqif
سوق واقف -: *Opening Hours* - 08:00-23:30 -: ***Cost per
person appx*** ***** -: *Phone* - +974 4411 1243 -: *Email* - -:
WebSite - www.thevillageqatar.com -: *Description* - Stylish
dining (there are three dining options in this location) just
outside the main Souq Waqif. There is another branch on
Salwa Rd GPS 25.265308, 51.498197 -: *Book reference
number* 14116

ARGAN -: *Type of Location* RESTAURANT -: ***GPS***
25.289281, 51.531201 -: *Street* - Al Jasra St, Doha, Qatar -:
Public Transport if available - Bus 76, 177 Metro Gold
Line Souq Waqif -: *Town / Area* - Souq Waqif سوق واقف -:
Opening Hours - 13:00-23:00 -: ***Cost per person appx***
****** -: *Phone* - +974 4433 6872 -: *Email* - -: *WebSite* -
https://www.tivolihotels.com/en/souq-waqif-al-jasra-
boutique-hotel/restaurants -: *Description* - Opulent
Moroccan restaurant with reasonably authentic dishes. -:
Book reference number 14126

**PARISA SOUQ WAQIF (ALSO AT SHARQ
VILLAGE)** -: *Type of Location* RESTAURANT -: ***GPS***

25.287756, 51.533261 -: *Street* - Inside Souq Waqif -: *Public Transport if available* - Bus 76, 177 Metro Gold Line Souq Waqif -: *Town / Area* - Souq Waqif سوق واقف -: *Opening Hours* - 12:00-00:00 -: **Cost per person appx** ****** -: *Phone* - +974 4441 1494 -: *Email* - dining.sharq@ritzcarlton.com -: *WebSite* - http://www.ritz-carlton.com/en/hotels/qatar/sharq-village/dining/parisa-souq-waqif -: *Description* - A destination in itself with decor imitating the Golestine Palace in Tehran, live music and excellent food, with a price reflecting it all. -: *Book reference number* 14150

TEA TIME -: *Type of Location* RESTAURANT -: **GPS** 25.287087, 51.533027 various locations (13+) in Qatar including Souq Waqif -: *Street* - -: *Public Transport if available* - -: *Town / Area* - Various -: *Opening Hours* - 24 Hours -: **Cost per person appx** * -: *Description* - a wide range of teas with all sorts of flavours -: *Book reference number* 14020

Other Restaurants near Al Corniche

AL MOURJAN -: *Type of Location* RESTAURANT -: **GPS** 25.307597, 51.519492 -: *Street* - Al Corniche -: *Public Transport if available* - Bus 76, 777 Metro Red Line Corniche -: *Town / Area* - Al Corniche الكورنيش -: *Opening Hours* - 12:00-00:00 -: **Cost per person appx** *** -: *Phone* - +974 4483 4423 -: *Email* - -: *Description* - Halfway along the Al Corniche in Balhambar building (the restaurant is often called by this name) . A comfortable mix of decor, with exterior seating on a cool evening or winter walk - an ideal stop. Light meal, soft drinks & snacks. You, of course, are paying for the view. -: *Book reference number* 14046

JW'S STEAKHOUSE (DOHA MARRIOTT) -:

Type of Location RESTAURANT -: **GPS** 25.286457, 51.562910 -: *Street* - Ras Abu Abboud Street -: *Public Transport if available* - Bus 76, 109 Metro Gold Line National Museum -: *Town / Area* - Al Corniche الكورنيش -: *Opening Hours* - 18:30-23:30 (Fri & Sat until 01:00) -: **Cost per person appx** ****** -: *Phone* - +974 4429 8499 -: *Email* - dinemarriottdoha@marriotthotels.com -: *WebSite* - https://www.marriott.com/hotel-restaurants/dohmc-doha-marriott-hotel/jw's-steak-house/91407/home-page.mi? -: *Description* - Smart casual creates a slight sense of occasion, which is reinforced by the food and service. -: *Book reference number* 14138

LAMZANI GRILL AND BRANCHES -: *Type of Location* RESTAURANT -: **GPS** 25.279941, 51.537014 -: *Street* - Ras Abu Abboud St -: *Public Transport if available* - Bus, many bus routes & about 500m south of Al Ghanim Bus Station. Metro Gold Line Souq Waqif or Red Line Al Doha Al Jadeda. -: *Town / Area* - Al Ghanim الغانم -: *Opening Hours* - 12:00-01:00 (Friday 14:30 -01:00) -: **Cost per person appx** * -: *Phone* - +974 55526345 (Mobile) -: *Email* - info@lamazani.com -: *WebSite* - www.lamazani.com -: *Description* - Busy, low cost Persian style kebab restaurant. -: *Book reference number* 14006

BEIRUT RESTAURANT (WITH BRANCHES) -: *Type of Location* RESTAURANT -: **GPS** 25.285022, 51.508900 -: *Street* - Al Jazeera St -: *Public Transport if available* - Bus 78, Metro Gold Line Al Saad -: *Town / Area* - Al Saad السد -: *Opening Hours* - 02:00- 13:00 yes - closed over lunchtime 15:00–23:30pm -: **Cost per person appx** ** -: *Phone* - +974 4435 5258 -: *Email* - info@beirutrest.com -: *WebSite* - www.beirutrest.com/ -:

Description - Simple well established, popular Lebanese restaurant. -: *Book reference number* 14034

C.MONDO (CENTRO CAPITAL HOTEL) IN AL JAZEERA ST -: *Type of Location* RESTAURANT -: *GPS* 25.284431, 51.511833 -: *Street* - Al Jazeera St -: *Public Transport if available* - Bus 78, Metro Gold Line Al Sadd - 1km away -: *Town / Area* - Fereej Bin Mahmoud فريج بن محمود -: *Opening Hours* - 12:00-02:00 -: *Cost per person appx* *** -: *Phone* - +974 4455 5111 -: *Email* - contact form -: *WebSite* - https://www.rotana.com/centrohotels/qatar/doha/centrocapitaldoha/dining -: *Description* - One of the more popular Bars in Doha, a younger crowd than some others. -: *Book reference number* 14050

MIZ BAR AND TERRACE (THE WESTIN DOHA) -: *Type of Location* RESTAURANT -: *GPS* 25.275305, 51.514136 -: *Street* - Salwa Rd -: *Public Transport if available* - Bus 49,304 Metro Gold Line Bin Mahmoud -: *Town / Area* - Fereej Bin Mahmoud فريج بن محمود -: *Opening Hours* - 17:00-02:00 (Sunday closes at 00:00) -: *Cost per person appx* *** -: *Phone* - +974 4492 1555 -: *Email* - -: *WebSite* - www.mixbardoha.com -: *Description* - Popular bar with indoor and terrace seating. -: *Book reference number* 14056

C.TASTE (CENTRO CAPITAL HOTEL) -: *Type of Location* RESTAURANT -: *GPS* 25.284431, 51.511833 -: *Street* - Al Jazeera St -: *Public Transport if available* - Bus 78, Metro Gold Line Al Sadd - 1km away -: *Town / Area* - Fereej Bin Mahmoud فريج بن محمود -: *Opening Hours* - 06:00-22:30 -: *Cost per person appx* **** -: *Phone* - T: +974 4455 5000 -: *Email* - centro.capital-doha@rotana.com -: *WebSite* - https://www.rotana.-

com/centrohotels/qatar/doha/centrocapitaldoha/dining   -:
Description - A limited but well produced menu from this
modern well run restaurant in the Centro Hotel. -: *Book
reference number* 14072

**DI CAPRI RISTORANTE (LA CIGALE
HOTEL)** -: *Type of Location* RESTAURANT -: **GPS**
25.280381, 51.507668 -: *Street* - , C Ring Rd /Suhaim Bin
Hamad Street -: *Public Transport if available* - Bus
32,42,78 Metro Gold Line Al Sadd -: *Town / Area* - Fereej
Bin Mahmoud فريج بن محمود -: *Opening Hours* - 11:30-
15:00 / 07:00 - 23:00 -: **Cost per person appx** **** -:
Phone - +97144288840 -: *Email* - info@lacigalehotel.com -:
WebSite - http://www.lacigalehotel.com/sub_catego-
ry.php?intCategoryId=4 -: *Description* - Vivid ambiance
with a hint of the late 1950s modern Italy. The food lives
up to the ambience. -: *Book reference number* 14074

SABI THAI (WESTIN HOTEL) -: *Type of Location* RESTAURANT -: **GPS** 25.275305, 51.514136 -:
Street - Salwa Rd -: *Public Transport if available* - Bus
49,304 Metro Gold Line Bin Mahmoud -: *Town / Area* -
Fereej Bin Mahmoud فريج بن محمود -: *Opening Hours* -
12:00 -15:00/18:30-23:00 -: **Cost per person appx**
***** -: *Phone* - +974 4492 1555 -: *Email* - dining.do-
ha@westin.com -: *WebSite* - www.sabaithaidoha.com -:
Description - Authentic Thai restaurant, though alcohol
offering could be improved. -: *Book reference number*
14108

**HUNTERS ROOM & GRILL (THE WESTIN
DOHA)** -: *Type of Location* RESTAURANT -: **GPS**
25.275305, 51.514136 -: *Street* - off Salwa Rd -: *Public
Transport if available* - Bus 49,304 -: *Town / Area* - Fereej
Bin Mahmoud فريج بن محمود -: *Opening Hours* - 12:00 -

16:00 19:00-23:00 -: **_Cost per person appx_** ****** -: _Phone_ - +974 3359 8514 -: _Email_ - dining.doha@west-in.com -: _WebSite_ - www.huntersdoha.com/ -: _Description_ - Potentially a good steak house, let down by inconsistent service. -: _Book reference number_ 14132

SEASONAL TASTES (WESTIN HOTEL) -: _Type of Location_ RESTAURANT -: **_GPS_** 25.275305, 51.514136 -: _Street_ - Salwa Rd -: _Public Transport if available_ - Bus 49,304 Metro Gold Line Bin Mahmoud -: _Town / Area_ - Fereej Bin Mahmoud فريج بن محمود -: _Opening Hours_ - 18:30-23:00 -: **_Cost per person appx_** ****** -: _Phone_ - +974 4492 1555 -: _Email_ - dining.doha@west-in.com -: _WebSite_ - www.seasonaltastesdoha.com/ -: _Description_ - International restaurant with nightly themed food nights -: _Book reference number_ 14156

PAK PAKWAN RESTAURANT -: _Type of Location_ RESTAURANT -: **_GPS_** 25.285841, 51.523389 -: _Street_ - Al Diwan St -: _Public Transport if available_ - Bus 40, 41,42,43,45,55,56, 100, 101,101,102x, 104 Metro Msheireb (Hub) -: _Town / Area_ - Msheireb مشيرب -: _Opening Hours_ - 11:30-23:30 (Friday 12:30-23:30) -: **_Cost per person appx_** * -: _Phone_ - +974 3382 2399 -: _Email_ - - : _Description_ - Busy with good value food and usually quick service. -: _Book reference number_ 14008

DOHA SOUTH & EAST

BEAR LAMP -: _Type of Location_ SCULPTURE -: **_GPS_** 25.261940, 51.613147 -: _Street_ - Duty Free -: _Public Transport if available_ - Bus 109, 727,737,747,757,777 Metro Red Line Hamid International Airport -: _Town / Area_ - Hamad International

Airport مطار حمد الدولي -: *Opening Hours* - 24 Hours -: *Description* - This giant sculpture of a Teddy Bear and lamp by Swiss artist Urs Fischer acts as a mascot to the airport and acts as a hub in the Duty Free area. -: *Book reference number* 15002

SMALL LIE -: *Type of Location* SCULPTURE -: **GPS** 25.261940, 51.613147 -: *Street* - Departures E -: *Public Transport if available* - Bus 109, 727,737,747,757,777 Metro Red Line Hamid International Airport -: *Town / Area* - Hamad International Airport مطار حمد الدولي -: *Opening Hours* - 24 Hours -: *Description* - Small Lie the oversize wooden marionette by Brian Donnelly is in Hamad Airport departures area E (below the moving walkway). -: *Book reference number* 15014

DRAGON MART AND CHINA MALL سوق التنين -: *Type of Location* SHOPPING MALL -: **GPS** 25.194233, 51.455365 -: *Street* - Junction of Industrial Area Rd and East Industrial Street north -: *Public Transport if available* - Bus 301, 20,21,32,33,57,300,302,304,737 -: *Town / Area* - Industrial Area منطقة صناعية -: *Opening Hours* - Numerous independent shops having individual times around 10:00-22:00 -: *WebSite* - -: *Description* - The is an extensive stretch of shops with products imported from the Far East. Building materials, fabrics, electronic all within a short walk of each other. This is a pile it high - sell it cheap area. As with Asian Town below this is far from a must visit - but for cheap, eclectic shopping it's difficult to beat. -: *Book reference number* 20014

ASIAN TOWN المدينة الاسيويه -: *Type of Location* SHOPPING MALL -: **GPS** 25.188685, 51.461231 -:

Street - Junction of Industrial Area Rd and East Industrial St -: *Public Transport if available* - Bus 20,21,32,33,57,300,302,304,737 -: *Town / Area* - Industrial Area منطقة صناعية -: *Opening Hours* - A variety of leisure, retail and dining options having different, but very long hours. -: *WebSite* -: *Description* - This is the general leisure area that serves the large area for expat labour, chiefly from the Indian Subcontinent. Here is a Cricket Stadium 25.190205, 51.461690, open-air concert theatre 25.186765, 51.464169, Cinemas, Supermarkets, low-cost restaurants. These offer services and products focused on the residents of the vast accommodation 'township' to its east. This area is far from a must see for a typical visitor, however it can't be beaten for value from money shopping, especially if you are looking for a massive range of products from the Indian sub-continent. -: *Book reference number* 20016

AL THUMAMA STADIUM -: *Type of Location* SPORT 2022 -: *GPS* 25.235285, 51.530590 -: *Street* - E Ring Road -: *Public Transport if available* - Bus 10 -: *Town / Area* - Al Thumama الثمامة -: *Opening Hours* - As per event -: *Description* - A stadium for the 2022 World Cup -: *Book reference number* 21004

AL AHLI SPORTS CLUB النادي الأهلي الرياض -: *Type of Location* SPORT FACILITY -: *GPS* 25.252359, 51.533690 -: *Street* - Junction Najma St and D Ring Rd. -: *Public Transport if available* - Bus 10,12, 727 -: *Town / Area* - Nuaija نعيجة -: *Opening Hours* - 08:00-22:00 -: **Entrance & cost** Per event -: *Phone* - 00974.40327777 -: *Email* - info@al-ahliclub.com -: *WebSite* - www.al-ahliclub.com -: *Description* - Qatar's oldest football club is unfortunately away from the town centre. A variety of facilities, including a swimming pool make it worthwhile checking out. -: *Book reference number* 22000

AZRAQ AT BANANA -: *Type of Location* RESTAU-RANT -: ***GPS*** 25.294898, 51.646007 -: *Street* - from Corniche 25.292010, 51.534803 -: *Public Transport if available* - Bus 76,777 (Airport), Metro Gold Line Souq Waqif & Ferry from Dhow Harbour 25.292135, 51.534429 -: *Town / Area* - Banana Island Doha Bay جزيرة بنانا -: *Opening Hours* - 06.30 -23.00 -: ***Cost per person appx*** *********** -: *Phone* - +974 4040 5050 -: *Email* - fbreservations.adoh@anantara.com -: *WebSite* - https://www.anan-tara.com/en/banana-island-doha/restaurants/azraq   -: *Description* - Choice of indoor or outdoor dining with a wide selection of cuisines and buffet -: *Book reference number* 14096

AL NAHHAM RESTAURANT AT BANANA ISLAND RESORT -: *Type of Location* RESTAURANT -: ***GPS*** 25.294898, 51.646007 -: *Street* - Banana Island -: *Public Transport if available* - Bus 76,777 (Airport), Metro Gold Line Souq Waqif & Ferry from Dhow Harbour 25.292135, 51.534429 -: *Town / Area* - Banana Island Doha Bay جزيرة بنانا -: *Opening Hours* - 13:00-17:00 / 19:00 - 17:00 -: ***Cost per person appx*** ************ -: *Phone* - +974 4040 5116 -: *Email* - fbreservations.adoh@anan-tara.com -: *WebSite* - https://www.anantara.com/en/ba-nana-island-doha/restaurants/al-nahham -: *Description* - A fresh, open dining area, Indoor or outdoor dining over-looking the sea. Premium prices, you should expect a premium experience -: *Book reference number* 14124

Q LOUNGE & RESTAURANT AT BANANA ISLAND -: *Type of Location* RESTAURANT -: ***GPS*** 25.294898, 51.646007 -: *Street* - Banana Island -: *Public*

Transport if available - Bus 76,777 (Airport), Metro Gold Line Souq Waqif & Ferry from Dhow Harbour 25.292135, 51.534429 -: *Town / Area* - Banana Island Doha Bay جزيرة بنانا -: *Opening Hours* - 06.30-10:30 / 12.00-23.30 -: **Cost per person appx** ****** -: *Phone* - +974 4040 5116 -: *Email* - fbreservations.adoh@anantara.com -: *WebSite* - https://www.anantara.com/en/banana-island-doha/restaurants/q-lounge-and-restaurant -: *Description* - Overlooking a pool, beach, sea and in the distance Doha's West Bay skyline, the food is also good. -: *Book reference number* 14152

RIVA AT BANANA ISLAND -: *Type of Location* RESTAURANT -: **GPS** 25.294898, 51.646007 -: *Street* - Banana Island -: *Public Transport if available* - Bus 76,777 (Airport), Metro Gold Line Souq Waqif & Ferry from Dhow Harbour 25.292135, 51.534429 -: *Town / Area* - Banana Island Doha Bay جزيرة بنانا -: *Opening Hours* - 13:00-22:00 (Closed Sunday) -: **Cost per person appx** ****** -: *Phone* - +974 4040 5116 -: *Email* - fbreservations.adoh@anantara.com -: *WebSite* - https://www.anantara.com/en/banana-island-doha/restaurants/riva -: *Description* - Overlooking the sea an excellent location for good food. -: *Book reference number* 14154

MEESH CAFÉ AT THE CROWNE PLAZA -: *Type of Location* RESTAURANT -: **GPS** 25.274010, 51.541511 -: *Street* - Al Matar St -: *Public Transport if available* - Bus 11,747, 11901, 12901 Metro Red Line Al Doha Al Jaded -: *Town / Area* - Najma نجمة -: *Opening Hours* - 24 Hours -: **Cost per person appx** ** -: *Phone* - 974 4408 7777 -: *Email* - -: *Description* - Good alternative to Starbucks and similar brands. -: *Book reference number* 14042

STOCK BURGER CO (HOLIDAY INN) -: *Type of Location* RESTAURANT -: *GPS* 25.273227, 51.542556 -: *Street* - Al Matar St -: *Public Transport if available* - Bus 11.747, 11901, 12901 Metro Al Doha Al Jadeda -: *Town / Area* - Najma نجمة -: *Opening Hours* - 12:00-02:00 -: *Cost per person appx* **** -: *Phone* - +974 4031 3333 -: *Email* - -: *WebSite* - www.ihg.com/holidayinn/hotels/gb/en/doha/dohbp/hoteldetail/dining#   -: *Description* - A mix of good burgers, alcohol and live sport coverage. -: *Book reference number* 14084

THE CELLAR (ORYX ROTANA) -: *Type of Location* RESTAURANT -: *GPS* 25.267965, 51.554113 -: *Street* - Al Nahda School St / C Ring Rd. -: *Public Transport if available* - Bus 94, 119, 129, 747, 757 Metro Red Line Umm Ghuwailina -: *Town / Area* - Umm Ghuwailina ام غويلينا -: *Opening Hours* - 12:00-02:00 -: *Cost per person appx* *** -: *Phone* - +974 4402 3454 -: *Email* - Contact Form -: *WebSite* - https://www.rotana.com/rotanahotelandresorts/qatar/doha/oryxrotana/diningout/thecellar/booknow -: *Description* - Limited food menu with reasonable alcohol menu. -: *Book reference number* 14060

AL NAFOURAH GARDEN -: *Type of Location* RESTAURANT -: *GPS* 25.267965, 51.554113 -: *Street* - Al Matar St -: *Public Transport if available* - 49,747, 11901,12901 -: *Town / Area* - Umm Ghuwailina ام غويلينا - : *Opening Hours* - 12:00-02:00 -: *Cost per person appx* **** -: *Phone* - +974 4402 3333 -: *Email* - -: *WebSite* - https://www.rotana.com/rotanahotelandresorts/qatar/doha/oryxrotana/diningout/alnafourahgarden -: *Description* - Largely outdoor dining with a comprehensive menu along with shisha (water pipe, hookah, hubbly bubbly). -: *Book reference number* 14064

PAPER MOON (1ST FLOOR JAIDAH SQUARE COMPLEX) -: *Type of Location* RESTAU-RANT -: *GPS* 25.273054, 51.544814 -: *Street* - Umm Ghuwailina St / Al Matar St -: *Public Transport if available* - Bus 747, 11901, 12901 Metro Red Line Umm Ghuwailina -: *Town / Area* - Umm Ghuwailina ام غويلينا -: *Opening Hours* - 11:30 - 22:45 -: *Cost per person appx* ***** -: *Phone* - +974 4016 6000 -: *Email* - info@paper-moondoha.com -: *WebSite* - www.papermoondoha.com/ -: *Description* - Comfortable modern style with option of indoor or outdoor tables. -: *Book reference number* 14106

JAZZ CLUB (ORYX ROTANA) -: *Type of Location* RESTAURANT -: *GPS* 25.267965, 51.554113 -: *Street* - off Al Matar St/ C Ring Rd -: *Public Transport if available* - Bus 94, 119, 129, 747, 757 Metro Red Line Umm Ghuwailina -: *Town / Area* - Umm Ghuwailina ام غويلينا -: *Opening Hours* - 17:00-02:00 (Closed Saturday) -: *Cost per person appx* ****** -: *Phone* - +974 4402 3444 -: *Email* - oryx@rotana.com -: *WebSite* - www.rotana.com/oryxrotana -: *Description* - A live band (not necessarily all jazz music) with light food and alcohol -: *Book reference number* 14136

EDUCATION CITY & DOHA WEST

AL WAJBAH FORT قلعة الوجبة -: *Type of Location* HISTORICAL -: *GPS* 25.301958, 51.394245 -: *Street* - south of Dukhan Rd. -: *Public Transport if available* - Bus 40,41,42,57 (2-kilometre walk) -: *Town / Area* - Al Wajbah الوجبة -: *Opening Hours* - not open. -: *Entrance & cost* not open -: *Description* - Built by the start of the 19thc this small fort is to the west of Doha's centre. The fort is a courtyard type with a range of rooms opening directly onto the courtyard. The general area is high security, so do ensure you adhere to non-photography of these and any prohibited notifications. -: *Book reference number* 10006

RAYYAN CASTLE قلعة الريان -: *Type of Location* HISTORICAL -: *GPS* 25.300634, 51.430827 -: *Street* - Al Rayyan Al Jadeed St (turn off the highway into Old Rayyan/Education City – the fort is to the west of the housing) -: *Public Transport if available* - Bus 57, 104,104a Metro Green Line Al Shaqab -: *Town / Area* - Al Rayyan الريان -: *Opening Hours* - not open. *Description* - Rayyan Castle is also known as Sheikh Ali bin Abdullah Fort. Sheikh Ali was the Amir of Qatar from 1949-1960. The fort is essentially a fortified residence, which then was outside Doha. The substantial wall, 180m on each side, enclosed a number of compounds. North of the fort is a secondary, modern, fortified building. Currently, Rayyan Fort is not open. -: *Book reference number* 10018

MATHAF ARAB MUSEUM OF MODERN ART المتحف العربي للفن الحديث -: *Type of Location* MUSEUM -: *GPS* 25.310460, 51.419488 -: *Street* - Al Luqta St via Gate 1 entrance -: *Public Transport if available* - No public transport -: *Town / Area* - Education City المدينة التعليمية -: *Opening Hours* – Sat - Thurs 09:00-19:00 Fri 13:30-19:00 -: *Entrance & cost* QAR50 / all Qatar Museum's tickets QAR100 (the organisation not a general pass this includes the Museum of Islamic Art, Mathaf and National Museum of Qatar – visit 3 for the price of 2) – tickets have a validity of three consecutive days from the date of initial admission - concessions for children and Qatar's residents -: *Phone* - +974 4402 8855 -: *Email* -

mathaf_info@qma.org.qa -: *WebSite* - www.mathaf.org.qa -: *Description* - The museum offers art workshops by regional and international tutors. Exhibitions are also held, principally of local artists. A substantial area of outdoor sculptures adds interest to a visit as does a selection from its permanent collection. A small gift shop and café add to the experience. This museum is in a relatively remote location in Doha, and this probably will only make it a must see to modern art fans. -: *Book reference number* 12604

VCU GALLERY (VIRGINIA COMMONWEALTH UNIVERSITY SCHOOL OF THE ARTS IN QATAR) جامعة فرجينيا كومنولث للفنون في قطر -:

Type of Location MUSEUM Art Gallery -: ***GPS*** 25.314692, 51.433561 -: *Street* - south of Al Luqta St -: *Public Transport if available* - No public transport -: *Town / Area* - Education City المدينة التعليمية -: *Opening Hours* - 09:00-12:00 Sun-Thurs -: ***Entrance & cost*** No Charge -: *Phone* - +974 4402 0555 -: *Email* - -: *WebSite* - www.qatar.vcu.edu -: *Description* - If you are in Education City, drop in here for a changing exhibition of student's art. -: *Book reference number* 12618

ASPIRE PARK حديقة اسباير -: *Type of Location* PUBLIC SPACE -: ***GPS*** 25.254813, 51.435536 -: *Street* - Al Waab St -: *Public Transport if available* - Bus 41,43,136,136a,137,137a,304 -: *Town / Area* - Aspire اسباير -: *Opening Hours* - 08:00-00:00 -: ***Entrance & cost*** No charge -: *Description* - Public park with large grassed areas and relatively mature trees. A lake is the principal feature. Some small cafes offer snacks. Very limited car parking for its size. -: *Book reference number* 12644

CINEMA QATAR -: *Type of Location* LEISURE -:

GPS 25.259277, 51.444534 -: *Street* - Junction Al Waab St and Aspire Park Rd -: *Public Transport if available* - Bus 31,32,136,136a,137,137a,301 Metro Al Aziziya (Villagio) - : *Town / Area* - Baaya / Aspire اسباير / بعيا -: *Opening Hours* - Check film screenings -: ***Entrance & cost*** per film -: *Phone* - -: *Email* - info@cinemaqatar.com -: *WebSite* - support@cinemaqatar.com -: *Description* - A Cinema within a shopping mall, with several screens, including iMax. Films in Qatar are censored potentially breaking plots. -: *Book reference number* 12000

MAMAN -: *Type of Location* SCULPTURE -: *GPS* 25.320840, 51.437663 -: *Street* - Qatar National Convention Centre, Al Luqta St -: *Public Transport if available* - No public transport -: *Town / Area* - Al Rayyan الريان -: *Opening Hours* - 24 Hours -: *Description* - Maman by Louise Bourgeois is a tribute to her mother in the form of a giant spider. It is one of six other mothers in locations including the Tate Modern London, National Gallery Canada and Crystal Bridges Museum in Arkansas. -: *Book reference number* 15008

PERCEVAL -: *Type of Location* SCULPTURE -: *GPS* 25.260330, 51.436412 -: *Street* - Aspire Park -: *Public Transport if available* - Bus 31,32,136,136a,137,137a,301 Metro Sports City -: *Town / Area* - Baaya / Aspire / بعيا اسباير -: *Opening Hours* - 24 Hours -: *Description* - Perceval by Sarah Lucas is a bronze life-size English shire horse and cart (with cement vegetable marrows), on the western side of the lake. -: *Book reference number* 15012

THE MIRACULOUS JOURNEY -: *Type of Location* SCULPTURE -: *GPS* 25.320803, 51.443855 -: *Street* - Sidra Medical and Research Centre exterior -: *Public Transport if available* - Metro Green Line Qatar National

Library -: *Town / Area* - Education City المدينة التعليمية -:
Opening Hours - 24 Hours -: *Description* - This series of 14
sculptures by Damien Hurst, portrays the development of a
baby, from conception to birth. These are true to life and
unmissable. In any city, they would attract controversy, as
they have done in Doha. -: *Book reference number* 15020

BRITISH COUNCIL QATAR المجلس البريطاني في
قطر -: *Type of Location* LEISURE LOCATION -: ***GPS***
25.2838112, 51.4832209 -: *Street* - Al Saad St -: *Public
Transport if available* - No public transport -: *Town / Area* -
Al Saad السد -: *Opening Hours* - 08:00-20:00 Sunday-
Thursday -: ***Entrance & cost*** -: *Phone* - +974 800 5501 -:
Email - general.enquiries@qa.britishcouncil.org -: *WebSite*
- www.britishcouncil.qa -: *Description* - Educational and
cultural organisation. A semi-government conduit for
British educational services -: *Book reference number* 30002

CENTRAL MARKET AREA السوق المركزي -: *Type
of Location* TOURIST SOUQ -: ***GPS*** 25.247512,
51.475609 -: *Street* - at the junction of Wholesale Market
St and Salwa Rd -: *Public Transport if available* - Bus
33,33a, 43,136, 136a,137.137a -: *Town / Area* - Abu
Hamour (Bu Hamour) بوهامور -: *Opening Hours* - 07:00-
21:00 -: ***Entrance & cost*** No Charge -: *Description* -
Until the mid 1990s the Central Markets area was on the
edge on the urban area of Doha, an ideal location for a
major 75 hectare wholesale market. Today urban sprawl
has included towns 8km, and more, west of the markets
within Doha's built up metropolis. The markets spread
south along Wholesale Market Rd and included (from
north at Salwa Rd to the south) a general market, the
'Omani' Souq (named because of the large number of
Omani merchants who set up business there in the 1950s);

several fruit and vegetable markets including date sales; a fish market; sheep & goat market; bird market; camel market and, separately, a slaughterhouse. The Doha municipal plant nursery finishes this row of flora and fauna oriented establishments. This area is oriented towards a wholesale/bulk buy customer, and the surroundings match the low cost of the produce. For a visitor, this is a remarkable insight into shopping for many of Qatar's residents. Though far from a 'must see' the size of the area does lend interest. -: *Book reference number* 30036

SOUQ AL ALI سوق العلي -: *Type of Location* TOURIST SOUQ -: *GPS* 25.318910, 51.470024 -: *Street* - Junction Khalifa St and Doha Expressway -: *Public Transport if available* - Bus 45 -: *Town / Area* - Al Luqta اللقطة -: *Opening Hours* - Independent shops various times. Most shops open between 10:00-12:00/16:00-22:00 and Restaurants from 10:00-22:00 - Ramadhan timings will vary. -: **Entrance & cost** No Charge -: *Description* - This is a low cost traditional, as in before the glitzy shopping malls, shopping area. A mix of shops with grocery, pet shops, clothing and fast food. Not a must see - but this is popular with locals -: *Book reference number* 30042

LANDMARK MALL -: *Type of Location* SHOPPING MALL -: *GPS* 25.333834, 51.467306 -: *Street* - Doha Expressway / Al Markhiya St -: *Public Transport if available* - Bus 100, 101 -: *Town / Area* - Al Duhail الدحيل -: *Opening Hours* - 09:00-22:00 -: *Phone* - +974 4487 5222 -: *Email* - info@landmarkdoha.com -: *WebSite* - www.landmarkdoha.com -: *Description* – one of several other large shopping malls with pharmacy, Virgin Megastore, Marks and Spencer, Carrefour and numerous other mid-price shops, mainly franchise. -: *Book reference number* 20006

VILLAGIGGIO MALL -: *Type of Location* SHOP-PING MALL -: *GPS* 25.259277, 51.444534 -: *Street* - Junction Al Waab St and Aspire Park Rd -: *Public Transport if available* - Bus 31,32,136,136a,137,137a,301 Metro Al Aziziya (Villagio) -: *Town / Area* - Baaya / Aspire / بعيا اسباير -: *Opening Hours* - 09:00-22:00 (Friday closed 11:00-12:30 prayer time) -: *Phone* - +974 4422 7400 -: *Email* - info@villaggioqatar.com -: *WebSite* - www.villaggioqatar.com/ -: *Description* - entertainment (boating canal, ice skating & more) and retail outlets including Virgin MegaStore, Carrefour, and mid-price brands -: *Book reference number* 20012

Villagio mall

GONDOLANIA ICE RINK & LEISURE

جوندولينيا للتزلج -: *Type of Location* LEISURE ACTIVITY -: ***GPS*** 25.259277, 51.444534 -: *Street* - Junction Al Waab St and Furosiya -: *Public Transport if available* - Bus 31,32,136,136a,137,137a,301 Metro Al Aziziya (Villagio) -: *Town / Area* - Baaya / Aspire اسباير / بعيا -: *Opening Hours* - 09:23:00 -: ***Entrance & cost*** up to QR150 -: *Phone* - 4403 9800 -: *Email* - info@gondolania.com -: *WebSite* - www.gondolania.com -: *Description* - Located inside Villagio mall this is an extensive indoor leisure area, focused on children. Given its name there has to be Gondolas, add in Go Karts from QR70, Ice Skating QR35 upwards, Laser Games from QR40, 10Pin Bowling, Roller Coaster and so on. Probably the most interesting Shopping Mall if you are a visitor to Doha. -: *Book reference number* 12010

QATAR EQUESTRIAN FEDERATION الاتحاد

القطري للفروسية -: *Type of Location* SPORT FACILITY -: ***GPS*** 25.283467, 51.430339 -: *Street* - Furousiya St -: *Public Transport if available* - Bus 40 or 43, 57 -: *Town / Area* - Muaither معيذر -: *Opening Hours* - 08:00-19:00 (closed Friday & Saturday) -: ***Entrance & cost*** Per event -: *Phone* - +974 4482 5708 -: *Email* - equestrainfederation2@olympic.qa -: *WebSite* - www.qefed.com -: *Description* - One of a small cluster of equestrian facilities. Here is dressage and show jumping -: *Book reference number* 22016

RACING & EQUESTRIAN CLUB نادي السباق

والفروسية -: *Type of Location* SPORT FACILITY -: ***GPS*** 25.278334, 51.427584 -: *Street* - Furousiya St -: *Public Transport if available* - Bus 43,67 -: *Town / Area* - Muaither معيذر -: *Opening Hours* - as per event -: ***Entrance & cost***

Per event -: *Phone* - +974 44825708 -: *Email* - info@qrec.-gov.qa -: *WebSite* - www.qrec.gov.qa -: *Description* - One of a small cluster of equestrian facilities. Here dressage and show jumping events are held from November - April, especially on Wednesday & Thursday from 16:00. There is a riding school z.alsheikh@qrec.gov.qa. -: *Book reference number* 22020

AL SHAQAB HORSE RACING ACADEMY

أكاديمية الشقب لسباق الخيل -: *Type of Location* LEISURE CULTURE -: **GPS** 25.306166, 51.439567 -: *Street* - Al Shaqab St -: *Public Transport if available* - Bus 42,57 Metro Green Line Al Shaqab -: *Town / Area* - Al Shaqab الشقب -: *Opening Hours* - Events As per schedule - normal working hours 09:00-15:30 (closed Friday & Saturday). Tours need to be booked in advance. -: ***Entrance & cost*** No Charge -: *Phone* - (+974) 4454 1992 -: *Email* - alshaqab-tours@qf.org.qa -: *WebSite* - www.alshaqab.com -: *Description* - Dressage and show jumping area with periodic events (see media or website). This academy is a state of the facility for riding with extensive, and expensive, stabling for Arabian and thoroughbred horses. Tours are available against a booking. Consider staying in Al Shaqab Hotel, within the grounds, a small hotel with comfortable accommodation and restaurant - a walk from the hotel block. https://www.amlak.com.qa/en/portfolio/al-shaqab-hotel/ Endurance horse racing is also held based from Qatar Endurance Village 24.967926, 51.506645 at Mesaieed south of Doha. Events are usually on Saturdays with a start in the early morning. The events are 100km+ so they last much of the day (with physical checks during the event). 4x4 vehicle is essential to view. If you contact the event organisers, they may be able to offer options to view. -: *Book reference number* 12506

ALI BIN HAMAD AL ATTIYAH ARENA -: *Type of Location* SPORT 2022 -: *GPS* 25.270055, 51.489924 -: *Street* - Al Nadi St -: *Public Transport if available* - Bus, 31,33a,34,136,136a,137,137a Metro Al Sudan -: *Town / Area* - Fereej Al Soudan فريج السودان -: *Opening Hours* - As per event -: -: *Phone* - +974 4032 5529 -: *Email* - -: *WebSite* - www.abha-arena.com -: *Description* - A multi-purpose indoor arena for handball, badminton, boxing, wrestling -: *Book reference number* 21008

KHALIFA INTERNATIONAL STADIUM -: *Type of Location* SPORT 2022 -: *GPS* 25.263593, 51.446589 -: *Street* - Al Waab St -: *Public Transport if available* - Bus 31, 32, 136, 136a, 137,137a,301 Metro Gold Line Sports City -: *Town / Area* - Baaya / Aspire بعيا اسباير / -: *Opening Hours* - As per event -: *Description* - A stadium for the 2022 World Cup with 40,000 seats open -: *Book reference number* 21010

QATAR FOUNDATION STADIUM -: *Type of Location* SPORT 2022 -: *GPS* 25.311312, 51.425748 -: *Street* - Al Rayyan Al Jadeed St -: *Public Transport if available* - No public transport on publication date - expect this to change close to 2022 -: *Town / Area* - Education City المدينة التعليمية -: *Opening Hours* - As per event -: *Description* - A stadium for the 2022 World Cup with 40,000 seats | Opening: 2021 -: *Book reference number* 21016

AL SAAD SPORTS نادي السد الرياضي -: *Type of Location* SPORT FACILITY -: *GPS* 25.266093, 51.482766 -: *Street* - off Al Nadi St -: *Public Transport if available* - Bus 31, 32 , 301 -: *Town / Area* - Fereej Al Soudan فريج السودان -: *Opening Hours* - 08:00-22:00 -:

Entrance & cost Per event -: *Phone* - +974 4444 8080 -:
Email - alsadd@mcs.gov.qa -: *WebSite* - www.al-sadd-
club.com -: *Description* - Local sports club (football based)
with swimming pool adjacent -: *Book reference number*
22004

Horse dressage

QATAR NATIONAL CONVENTION CENTRE مركز قطر الوطني للمؤتمرات -: *Type of Location*
LEISURE CULTURE -: ***GPS*** 25.320633, 51.437452 -:
Street - Al Luqta St/ Dukhan Highway -: *Public Transport
if available* - Metro Green Line Qatar National Library -:
Town / Area - Education City المدينة التعليمية -: *Opening
Hours* - as per events -: ***Entrance & cost*** No Charge -:
Phone - +974 4470 7000 -: *Email* - sales@qncc.qa -:
WebSite - www.qncc.qa -: *Description* - This is a substan-
tial modern convention centre. Exhibition halls, modern
auditoriums for conferences as well as entertainment

events with smaller halls and rooms offer space for smaller events such as board meetings. Concerts of various types are held here in the smaller halls with information & ticket sales from www.qatarphilharmonicorchestra.org. Parking availability is substantial with a quoted 2,800 spaces (many of which are used by staff), also there are direct Metro links (NECC), good Bus options and of course Taxis offer flexible options. -: *Book reference number* 12514

QATAR NATIONAL LIBRARY متاحف مشيرب -: *Type of Location* LEISURE CULTURE -: ***GPS*** 25.318913, 51.441693 -: *Street* - Al Luqta St -: *Public Transport if available* - Bus 42,57 Metro Green Line Al Shaqab -: *Town / Area* - Education City المدينة التعليمية -: *Opening Hours* - Saturday – Thursday: 8:00 AM - 8:00 PM Fridays: 4:00 PM - 8:00 PM -: ***Entrance & cost*** No Charge -: *Phone* - +974 4454 6039 -: *Email* - qnl@qnl.qa -: *WebSite* - www.qnl.qa -: *Description* - A very substantial several story, state of the art modern library. Plenty of space to sit and research. Car parking with a shuttle bus is here 25.313704, 51.438175 -: *Book reference number* 12516

EDUCATION CITY GOLF CLUB نادي مدينة التعليمي للجولف -: *Type of Location* SPORT FACILITY -: ***GPS*** 25.303016, 51.422245 -: *Street* - Al Rayyan Al Jadeed St -: *Public Transport if available* - Bus 40, 104,104a -: *Town / Area* - Education City المدينة التعليمية -: *Opening Hours* - 07:00-17:00 -: ***Entrance & cost*** Per event -: *Phone* - +974 7773 7973 -: *Email* - Info@ecgolf.com -: *WebSite* - www.ecgolf.com -: *Description* - New course 18 hole golf course (+ short course) -: *Book reference number* 22012

JOES CRAB SHACK (TAWAR MALL) -: *Type of*

Location RESTAURANT -: **GPS** 25.336053, 51.480876 -
: *Street* - Arab League St/Al Markhiya St -: *Public Transport if available* - Bus 100, 101, 102,170,172 -: *Town /
Area* - Al Duhail South جنوب الدحيل -: *Opening Hours* -
12:30-22:00 (Fri 13:00-23:00) -: **Cost per person appx**
** -: *Phone* - +974 4039 2971 -: *Email* - -: *WebSite* -
www.joescrabshack.com/ -: *Description* - A franchise on 1st
floor in a relatively new mall. Worthwhile to try as an alternative to the big fast-food brands -: *Book reference number*
14040

SHAWARMA TIME (QATAR PETROLEUM SERVICE STATION) -: *Type of Location* RESTAU-

RANT -: **GPS** 25.34973, 51.456829 -: *Street* - Doha
Expressway (Al Shamal Road) /Al Khafji St -: *Public Transport if available* - Bus 102, 170 -: *Town / Area* - Al Duheil
الدحيل -: *Opening Hours* - 12:00-02:00 -: **Cost per
person appx** * -: *Phone* - +974 4455 1151 -: *Email* - -:
Description - shawarma style takeaway with limited seating,
ideal for takeaway. -: *Book reference number* 14016

AFGHAN BROTHERS (ONE OF SEVEN BRANCHES - ALL ARE COMPARABLE) -: *Type of

Location* RESTAURANT -: **GPS** 25.273263, 51.495824 -
: *Street* - Al Mirqab al Jadeed St -: *Public Transport if available* - Bus 49,94 Metro Joaan Metro 1km over busy rd. -:
Town / Area - Al Mirqab المرقاب -: *Opening Hours* - 07:00-
01:00 -: **Cost per person appx** * -: *Phone* - +974 4488
8556 -: *Email* - Alnasr@afghanbrothers.com -: *WebSite* -
www.afghanbrothers.com -: *Description* - Very good value
Afghani (& Pakistani) meat and rice-based style food. Might
only have spoons, ask for knife and fork if preferred. Take
away also available as is assorted Afghani sweets. -: *Book
reference number* 14000

TURKEY CENTRAL RESTAURANT -: *Type of Location* RESTAURANT -: *GPS* 25.273587, 51.496320 -: *Street* - Al Mirqab Al Jadeed St -: *Public Transport if available* - Bus 41, 94, Metro Gold Line Joaan -: *Town / Area* - Al Mirqab المرقاب -: *Opening Hours* - 11:00-01:00 -: **Cost per person appx** ** -: *Phone* - +974 4443 2927 -: *Description* - Substantial restaurant, relatively low cost. -: *Book reference number* 14044

AL MANDARIN RESTAURANT -one of several branches that mainly offer good fresh fruit juices

-: *Type of Location* RESTAURANT -: *GPS* 25.272492, 51.508848 -: *Street* - C Ring Rd / Salwa Rd -: *Public Transport if available* - Bus 49, 304 -: *Town / Area* - Al Nasr النصر -: *Opening Hours* - 24 Hours -: **Cost per person appx** * -: *Phone* - +974 4442 0808 -: *Description* - Good Value restaurant, other branches (not listed here) for example in Souq Waqif have Fresh Juice only. -: *Book reference number* 14002

AL SULTAN RESTAURANT - AL SAAD -: *Type of Location* RESTAURANT -: *GPS* 25.274297, 51.505279 -: *Street* - Al Mirqab Al Jadeed -: *Public Transport if available* - Bus 49, Metro Gold Line Al Saad -: *Town / Area* - Al Nasr النصر -: *Opening Hours* - 08:00-23:00 -: **Cost per person appx** ** -: *Phone* - +974 4441 1865 -: *Email* - info@al-sultanrestaurant.com -: *WebSite* - www.al-sultanrestaurant.com/ -: *Description* - Good value Lebanese restaurant (one of two in a chain) with selection of fruit juices -: *Book reference number* 14028

OCEAN BASKET (MALL OF QATAR) -: *Type of Location* RESTAURANT -: *GPS* 25.324452, 51.349969 -: *Street* - Dukhan Highway / National Day Ceremonial Road (a complicated junction) -: *Public Transport if avail-

able - Bus 104, 104A from Al Ghanim Bus Station -: *Town / Area* - Al Rayyan الريان -: *Opening Hours* - 11:00-23:00 (Friday 01:00-23:00) -: ***Cost per person appx*** ******** -: *Phone* - +974 4490 2944 -: *WebSite* - www.qatar.oceanbasket.com/ -: *Description* - Reasonable option if visiting Mall of Qatar. -: *Book reference number* 14078

SAJ BOUTIQUE -: *Type of Location* RESTAURANT -: ***GPS*** 25.269617, 51.476856 -: *Street* - Al Waab St / Al Bustan St -: *Public Transport if available* - Bus 32,41,304 Metro Gold Line Gold Line Al Sudan -: *Town / Area* - Al Saad السد -: *Opening Hours* - 07:00-01:00 -: ***Cost per person appx*** ***** -: *Phone* - +974 6607 8444 -: *Description* - shawarma type takeaway with better ingredients than many other similar outlets, with small seating area. -: *Book reference number* 14014

ATRIUM LOUNGE -: *Type of Location* RESTAURANT -: ***GPS*** 25.283564, 51.495877 -: *Street* - Al Manara St, Jawaan St, -: *Public Transport if available* - Bus 32,41,49, 78,94,304, Metro Gold Line Joaan -: *Town / Area* - Al Saad السد -: *Opening Hours* - 07:00-23:30 -: ***Cost per person appx*** ******** -: *Phone* - +974 4 424 7777 -: *Email* - info.mdoh@millenniumhotels.com -: *WebSite* - https://www.millenniumhotels.com/en/doha/millennium-hotel-doha/atrium/ -: *Description* - A good choice for a light meal if in the area . -: *Book reference number* 14070

THREE SIXTY (360) TORCH DOHA -: *Type of Location* RESTAURANT -: ***GPS*** 25.262017, 51.444912 -: *Street* - off Al Waab Street, Al Buwairda St -: *Public Transport if available* - 31,32,40, 136,137,301,306. Metro Gold Line Sport City -: *Town / Area* - Baaya / Aspire / بعيا اسباير -: *Opening Hours* - 12:00-15:00 / 19:00-23:00 -: ***Cost per person appx*** ********** -: *Phone* - +974 4446

5600 -: *Email* - reservation@thetorchdoha.com -: *WebSite* - www.thetorchdoha.com.qa -: *Description* - Mediterranean & seafood restaurant (no alcohol) set on the 47th floor of The Torch. The food is good but what makes this outstanding is the revolving view - best enjoyed at 19:00 (arrive early to catch the skyscraper lights coming on 8km away). Very Smart Casual, or suit & dress (appropriate national dress). The other restaurants in this hotel are also good, but as it's out of the way, the revolving restaurant does make it worth the journey. The most distinctive hotel in Doha opened for Asian Games; the restaurants are distinctive and all worth a visit, especially 360. -: *Book reference number* 14162

SHEBESTAN PALACE RESTAURANT -: *Type of Location* RESTAURANT -: *GPS* 25.280858, 51.503922 -: *Street* - Al Saad St -: *Public Transport if available* - Bus 31,32, 301 Metro Gold Line Al Saad -: *Town / Area* - Mirqab Al Jadeed المرقاب الجديد -: *Opening Hours* - 12:00-00:00 -: *Cost per person appx* **** -: *Phone* - +974 4432 1555 -: *Description* - Extremely well established restaurant, decor less overwhelming than other Persian options in Doha. The food and service are also less overwhelming, though at a lower price. -: *Book reference number* 14082

WRAP IT - in food court of several shopping malls, Gulf Mall, Landmark etc -: *Type of Location* RESTAURANT -: *GPS* 25.333834, 51.467306 various locations in Qatar -: *Street* - -: *Public Transport if available* - -: *Town / Area* - Various -: *Opening Hours* - 09:00-23:30 (or as in specific food court opening hours) -: *Cost per person appx* * -: *Phone* - -: *Description* - The Gulfs most popular snack the shawarma, branded here as Wrap-it -: *Book reference number* 14024

West Bay

WEST BAY

CITY CENTRE DOHA -: *Type of Location* SHOPPING MALL -: ***GPS*** 25.325879, 51.530399 -: *Street* - Conference Centre, Omar Al Mukhtar -: *Public Transport if available* - Bus 57,74,76,777 Metro Doha Exhibition and Convention Center (DECC) -: *Town / Area* - West Bay الخليج الغربي -: *Opening Hours* - 10:00-22:00 (Friday closed 11:00-13:00) -: *Phone* - +974 4493 3355 -: *Email* - Contact Form -: *WebSite* - www.citycenterdoha.com/ -: *Description* - Doha Exhibition and Conference Centre, numerous hotels, a few government ministries. A major shopping mall on five floors. It is undergoing a complete renovation, though still open. Banks, Carrefour supermarket, food court, children's entertainment centre, ice skating are all tenants. Despite the name - this is not one of the Al Futtaim City Centres. -: *Book reference number* 20000

ICE SKATING RINK ساحة التزلج -: *Type of Location* LEISURE ACTIVITY -: ***GPS*** 25.325857, 51.530053 -: *Street* - Junction of Omar Al Mukhtar Rd and Conference Centre Rd -: *Public Transport if available* - Bus 57 Metro Doha Exhibition and Convention Centre (DECC) -: *Town / Area* - West Bay الخليج الغربي -: *Opening Hours* - 10:00-22:00 -: ***Entrance & cost*** currently closed for refurbishment -: *Phone* - -: *Description* - Ice Skating within the atrium of a Shopping Mall. As it's a peripheral service for the mall maintenance and management are below the level of similar facilities in other major cities. -: *Book reference number* 12014

QATAR SPORTS CLUB, SUHEIM BIN HAMAD STADIUM, QATAR HANDBALL FEDERATION نادي قطر الرياضي -: *Type of Location* SPORT FACILITY -: ***GPS*** 25.316760, 51.513532 -: *Street* - Junction Al Istiqlal St and Al Markhiya St -: *Public Transport if available* - Bus 75, 100,101,102,102X,170 Metro Red Line 1500metres walk -: *Town / Area* - Al Dafna الدفنة -: *Opening Hours* - 08:00-22:00 -: ***Entrance & cost*** Per event -: *Phone* - +965 9733 0415 -: *Email* - info@qatarsc.com -: *WebSite* - www.qatarsc.com/ -: *Description* - A sports complex focused on one of Qatar's more successful league teams. Regular local football matches are held, check for a detailed schedule in the media. Parking is very limited, so if the match is a major event, a taxi is a good option to use. -: *Book reference number* 22018

ROYAL ISTANBUL RESTAURANT (BEHIND WEST BAY PETROL STATION) -: *Type of Location* RESTAURANT -: ***GPS*** 25.325905, 51.517153 -: *Street* - Al Istiqal St / Al Intisar -: *Public Transport if available* -

Bus 78 -: *Town / Area* - Al Dafna الدفنة -: *Opening Hours* - 11:00-00:00 -: ***Cost per person appx*** * -: *Phone* - +974 4498 1268 -: *Email* - RoyalIstanbul@BakeMartDoha.com - : *Description* - Simple Turkish Food, which is popular with good takeaway service. -: *Book reference number* 14012

GORDON RAMSAY AT THE ST. REGIS -: *Type of Location* RESTAURANT -: ***GPS*** 25.350277, 51.528766 -: *Street* - off Lusail Express -: *Public Transport if available* - No public transport -: *Town / Area* - Katara / West Bay الخليج الغربي / كتارا -: *Opening Hours* - 18:00-23:00 (Closed Sunday) -: ***Cost per person appx*** ****** - : *Phone* - +974 4446 0105 -: *Email* - dining.reservations@stregis.com -: *WebSite* - www.gordonramsaydoha.com -: *Description* - Simple décor and a modern take on Mediterranean, that is generally excellent, along with alcohol appropriate to the cuisine. -: *Book reference number* 14128

HAKKASAN (ST. REGIS DOHA) -: *Type of Location* RESTAURANT -: ***GPS*** 25.350277, 51.528766 -: *Street* - east of Lusail Highway -: *Public Transport if available* - No public transport -: *Town / Area* - Katara / West Bay الخليج الغربي / كتارا -: *Opening Hours* - 19:00-23:30 (also weekends 13:00-16:00) wine bar (18:00-01:00) -: ***Cost per person appx*** ****** -: *Phone* - +974 4446 0170 -: *Email* - reservation.hakkasan@stregis.com -: *WebSite* - www.hakkasan.com/locations/hakkasan-doha/ -: *Description* - Smart casual with restrictions on children below 11. The restaurant does operate a restrictive door policy - booking for tables advised. This restaurant is probably the most expensive Doha; it's reasonable to expect perfection = booking advised -: *Book reference number* 14130

VINE (ST REGIS) -: *Type of Location* RESTAU-
RANT -: *GPS* 25.350277, 51.528766 -: *Street* - off Lusail
Highway -: *Public Transport if available* - No public transport -: *Town / Area* - Katara / West Bay كتارا / الخليج الغربي
-: *Opening Hours* - 06:00-11:00/18:00-23:00 and Friday
(12:30-16:00) -: *Cost per person appx* ****** -: *Phone* -
+974 4446 0105 -: *Email* - dining.reservations@stregis.com
-: *WebSite* - www.vinedoha.com/ -: *Description* - elegant
restaurant with spacious interior and options to dine
outside. -: *Book reference number* 14166

**HAWAK CAFÉ (1ST FLOOR THE GATE
MALL)** -: *Type of Location* RESTAURANT -: *GPS*
25.323446, 51.526326 -: *Street* - Omar Al Mukhtar St -:
Public Transport if available - Bus 57, Metro Red Line
Doha Exhibition & Conference Centre (DECC) -: *Town /
Area* - West Bay الخليج الغربي -: *Opening Hours* - 08:00-
19:00 (Friday closes at 11:00-12:30) -: *Cost per person
appx* ** -: *Phone* - +974 4020 6214 -: *Description* - Attractive small café set inside one of Doha's more upmarket
shopping malls. -: *Book reference number* 14038

CHAMPIONS SPORTS BAR -: *Type of Location*
RESTAURANT -: *GPS* 25.324729, 51.527852 -: *Street* -
Omar Al Mukhtar -: *Public Transport if available* - Bus 57,
Metro Red Line Doha Exhibition & Conference Centre
(DECC) -: *Town / Area* - West Bay الخليج الغربي -: *Opening
Hours* - 16:00-02:00 -: *Cost per person appx* *** -:
Phone - -: *Description* – one of the better bars in Doha,
focused as its name suggest on live sports TV-: *Book refer-
ence number* 14052

W CAFÉ (W HOTEL) -: *Type of Location*
RESTAURANT -: *GPS* 25.328356, 51.530124 -: *Street* -
Diplomatic St -: *Public Transport if available* - Bus

57,74,76,777 Metro Doha Exhibition and Convention Centre (DECC Consider the , paid, shuttle coach services the general West Bay area every 15mins for all West Bay Hotels -: *Town / Area* - West Bay الخليج الغربي -: *Opening Hours* - 07:00-00:00 (Friday from 08:00) -: **Cost per person appx** *** -: *Phone* - +974 4453 5135 -: *Email* - bnfreservations.wdoha@whotels.com -: *WebSite* - www.w-cafedoha.com -: *Description* - An good alternative to Starbucks at not much more cost. -: *Book reference number* 14062

APPLEBEE'S (CHAIN) -: *Type of Location* RESTAURANT -: **GPS** 25.325806, 51.530499 -: *Street* - Conference Centre -: *Public Transport if available* - Bus 78,Metro Doha Exhibition and Convention Centre (DECC) -: *Town / Area* - West Bay الخليج الغربي -: *Opening Hours* - 10:00-23:00 -: **Cost per person appx** **** -: *Phone* - +974 4493 4880 -: *Email* - contact form -: *WebSite* - www.applebeesme.com/qatar/ -: *Description* - Part of the Applebee franchise, one of several branches in Doha. American style ribs and fast food options. Predictable good food quality and efficient service. -: *Book reference number* 14066

AQUA LOUNGE -: *Type of Location* RESTAURANT -: **GPS** 25.325806, 51.530499 -: *Street* - Conference Centre -: *Public Transport if available* - Bus 78, Metro Doha Exhibition and Convention Centre (DECC) -: *Town / Area* - West Bay الخليج الغربي -: *Opening Hours* - 18:00-23:00 -: **Cost per person appx** **** -: *Phone* - +974 4419 5000 -: *WebSite* - http://www.marriottmarquisdoha-dining.com/restaurant/hotels/hotel-information/travel/dohmq/restaurant.aspx? -: *Description* - Poolside bar overlooked by the skyline of Doha, which is especially dramatic at night. -: *Book reference number* 14068

OLIVE OIL ROTANA CITY CENTRE -: *Type of Location* RESTAURANT -: *GPS* 25.324391, 51.532985 -: *Street* - Diplomatic St / Conference Centre St -: *Public Transport if available* - Bus 74,777 Metro Red Line Doha Exhibition & Conference Centre (DECC) -: *Town / Area* - West Bay الخليج الغربي -: *Opening Hours* - 06:30-23:30 -: *Cost per person appx* **** -: *Phone* - +974 4445 8727 -: *Email* - Contact Form -: *WebSite* - https://www.rotana.com/rotanahotelandresorts/qatar/doha/citycentrerotanadoha/diningout/oliveoil/booknow -: *Description* - International buffet offering a good choice in West Bay - convenient to the conference centre and City Centre Mall. -: *Book reference number* 14080

AL SULTAN BRAHIM -: *Type of Location* RESTAURANT -: *GPS* 25.349435, 51.530946 -: *Street* - off Lusail Highway -: *Public Transport if available* - Metro Red Line Al Qassar -: *Town / Area* - West Bay الخليج الغربي -: *Opening Hours* - 12:00–16:30pm 18:30–23:30pm -: *Cost per person appx* ***** -: *Phone* - +97444460000 -: *Email* - dining.reservations@stregis.com -: *WebSite* - www.alsultanbrahimdoha.com -: *Description* - Seafood near, but not on, the sea. The gardens are attractive to dine in, while the interior decor is almost bland. Make your choice of fish from the display. -: *Book reference number* 14094

BOSTON'S -: *Type of Location* RESTAURANT -: *GPS* 25.325812, 51.530540 -: *Street* - Omar Al Mukhtar / Conference Centre -: *Public Transport if available* - Bus 78,Metro Doha Exhibition and Convention Centre (DECC) -: *Town / Area* - West Bay الخليج الغربي -: *Opening*

Hours - 17:00-02:00 -: ***Cost per person appx*** ***** -: *Phone* - +974 4445 8888 -: *Email* - fb.citycentre@Rotana.com -: *WebSite* - www.rotanatimes.com/citycentrerotanadoha/dining/1368 -: *Description* - Popular modern pub style restaurant, with live sports. -: *Book reference number* 14098

LA SPIGA BY PAPER MOON (W DOHA) -:
Type of Location RESTAURANT -: ***GPS*** 25.328356, 51.530124 -: *Street* - Diplomatic St -: *Public Transport if available* - Bus 57,74,76,777 Metro Doha Exhibition and Convention Centre (DECC Consider the , paid, shuttle coach services the general West Bay area every 15mins for all West Bay Hotels -: *Town / Area* - West Bay الخليج الغربي -: *Opening Hours* - 12:00 - 16:00 / 17:00-00:00 -: ***Cost per person appx*** ***** -: *Phone* - +974 4453 5135 -: *Email* - bnfreservations.wdoha@whotels.com -: *WebSite* - www.laspigadoha.com -: *Description* - small stylish Italian restaurant with appropriate wine bar and smart casual dress -: *Book reference number* 14102

SRIDAN -: *Type of Location* RESTAURANT -: ***GPS*** 25.325056, 51.532927 -: *Street* - Conference Centre/Diplomatic St -: *Public Transport if available* - Bus 74 , 777 Metro Doha Exhibition and Convention Centre (DECC). -: *Town / Area* - West Bay الخليج الغربي -: *Opening Hours* - 6.00am – 10.30am / 12.00noon – 3.00pm / 6.00pm – 10.00pm -: ***Cost per person appx*** ***** -: *Phone* - +974 4429 5000 -: *Email* - Contact Form -: *WebSite* - http://www.shangri-la.com/doha/shangrila/dining/restaurants/sridan/ -: *Description* - Comfortable restaurant with a convenient location for DECC -: *Book reference number* 14112

TEATRO -: *Type of Location* RESTAURANT -:

GPS 25.324085, 51.533348 -: *Street* - Conference Centre -: *Public Transport if available* - Bus 74,777 Metro Red Line Doha Exhibition & Conference Centre (DECC) -: *Town / Area* - West Bay الخليج الغربي -: *Opening Hours* - 12:30-02:00 am (Friday and Saturday from 17:00) -: ***Cost per person appx*** ***** -: *Phone* - +974 4445 8888 -: *Email* - contact form -: *WebSite* - https://www.rotana.com/rotanahotelandresorts/qatar/doha/citycentrerotanadoha/diningout/teatro/booknow -: *Description* - Good option for a light meal with good range of alcohol -: *Book reference number* 14114

TRADER VIC'S (HILTON) -: *Type of Location* RESTAURANT -: ***GPS*** 25.327042, 51.541126 -: *Street* - Diplomatic St -: *Public Transport if available* - Bus 74 , 777 Metro Doha Exhibition and Convention Centre (DECC Consider the , paid, shuttle coach services the general West Bay area every 15mins for all West Bay Hotels -: *Town / Area* - West Bay الخليج الغربي -: *Opening Hours* - 16:00-02:00 (Friday from 13:00) -: ***Cost per person appx*** ***** -: *Phone* - +974 4423 3118 -: *WebSite* - www.tradervicsdoha.com/ -: *Description* - Part of the established chain. Smart Casual - overlooking the sea -: *Book reference number* 14118

WAHM (W HOTEL) -: *Type of Location* RESTAURANT -: ***GPS*** 25.328356, 51.530124 -: *Street* - Diplomatic St -: *Public Transport if available* - Bus 57,74,76,777 Metro Doha Exhibition and Convention Centre (DECC Consider the , paid, shuttle coach services the general West Bay area every 15mins for all West Bay Hotels -: *Town / Area* - West Bay الخليج الغربي -: *Opening Hours* - 17:00-02:00 -: ***Cost per person appx*** ***** -: *Phone* - +974 4453 5135 -: *Email* - bnfreservations.wdoha@whotels.com

-: *WebSite* - www.wahmdoha.com -: *Description* - Light food and bar with live music. -: *Book reference number* 14120

IPANEMA RODIZIO STYLE (MARRIOT MARQUIS HOTEL) -: *Type of Location* RESTAU-RANT -: *GPS* 25.324729, 51.527852 -: *Street* - Omar Al Mukhtar -: *Public Transport if available* - Bus 57, Metro Red Line Doha Exhibition & Conference Centre (DECC) -: *Town / Area* - West Bay الخليج الغربي -: *Opening Hours* - 18:30-23:00 (plus Friday 12:30-17:00) -: **Cost per person appx** ****** -: *Phone* - +974 4419 5000 -: *WebSite* - http://www.marriottmarquisdohadining.com/restaurant/hotels/hotel-information/travel/dohmq/restaurant.aspx?id=010 -: *Description* - Remarkably good venue, with good food, range of alcohol and often live music. -: *Book reference number* 14134

MARKET BY JEAN-GEORGES -: *Type of Location* RESTAURANT -: *GPS* 25.328356, 51.530124 -: *Street* - Diplomatic St -: *Public Transport if available* - Bus 57,74,76,777 Metro Doha Exhibition and Convention Centre (DECC Consider the , paid, shuttle coach services the general West Bay area every 15mins for all West Bay Hotels -: *Town / Area* - West Bay الخليج الغربي -: *Opening Hours* - 06:00-11:00/12:00-16:00/17:00-23:30 (Friday 12:00-16:00/17:00-23:30) -: **Cost per person appx** ****** -: *Phone* - +97444535135 -: *Email* - bnfreservations.wdoha@whotels.com -: *WebSite* - www.marketdoha.com -: *Description* - Simple European design ambiance, with a similar approach to the quality food. -: *Book reference number* 14140

NOBU -: *Type of Location* RESTAURANT -: *GPS* 25.323374, 51.541242 -: *Street* - Diplomatic St (Four

Seasons Marina) -: *Public Transport if available* - Bus 74,777 Metro Red Line Doha Exhibition & Conference Centre (DECC) -: *Town / Area* - West Bay الخليج الغربي -: *Opening Hours* - 18:00-01:00 (Friday 12:30-16:00) -: **Cost per person appx** ****** -: *Phone* - +974 4494 8600 -: *Email* - contact form -: *WebSite* - www.fourseasons.-com/doha/dining/restaurants/nobu_doha/ -: *Description* - Worth visiting for the views, the service and food don't quite match the price. -: *Book reference number* 14146

SHANGHAI CLUB (LEVEL 43 SHANGRI-LA HOTEL) -: *Type of Location* RESTAURANT -: *GPS* 25.324955, 51.533428 -: *Street* - Diplomatic St/ Conference Centre -: *Public Transport if available* - 57,74,76, 78,777 Metro Doha Exhibition and Convention Centre (DECC). -: *Town / Area* - West Bay الخليج الغربي -: *Opening Hours* - 12.30-16.00/ 18.30-23.30 -: **Cost per person appx** ****** -: *Phone* - +(974) 4429 5050 -: *Email* - shanghaiclub.sldh@shangri-la.com -: *WebSite* - http://www.shangri-la.com/doha/shangrila/dining/restaurants/shanghai-club/ -: *Description* - Smart evening dress code, with views of Doha Bay and good wine menu and occasional live music -: *Book reference number* 14158

SPICE MARKET (W DOHA) -: *Type of Location* RESTAURANT -: *GPS* 25.328356, 51.530124 -: *Street* - Diplomatic St -: *Public Transport if available* - Bus 57,74,76,777 Metro Doha Exhibition and Convention Centre (DECC Consider the , paid, shuttle coach services the general West Bay area every 15mins for all West Bay Hotels -: *Town / Area* - West Bay الخليج الغربي -: *Opening Hours* - 12:00-16:00/17:00-00:00 -: **Cost per person appx** ****** -: *Phone* - +974 4453 5000 -: *Email* - contact form -: *WebSite* - www.spicemarketdoha.com -: *Description*

- A cheerful ambiance with excellent meal selection. -: *Book reference number* 14160

ZENGO (KEMPINSKI RESIDENCES) -: *Type of Location* RESTAURANT -: *GPS* 25.328270, 51.531038 -: *Street* - off Diplomatic St -: *Public Transport if available* - Bus 74 , 777 Metro Doha Exhibition and Convention Centre (DECC Consider the , paid, shuttle coach services the general West Bay area every 15mins for all West Bay Hotels -: *Town / Area* - West Bay الخليج الغربي -: *Opening Hours* - 12:30-00:00 (Closed Saturday) -: *Cost per person appx* ****** -: *Phone* - +974 4453 5135 -: *Email* - Zengo@zengodoha.com -: *WebSite* - www.zengodoha.com -: *Description* - Asian menu with good alcohol selection. Ask for a window table to enjoy the view from 61st floor across Doha Bay to The Pearl -: *Book reference number* 14168

LALIGA LOUNGE (SHERATON HOTEL GROUNDS) -: *Type of Location* RESTAURANT -: *GPS* 25.319947, 51.534043 -: *Street* - Diplomatic St -: *Public Transport if available* - Bus 777 Metro Red Line Doha Exhibition & Conference Centre (DECC) -: *Town / Area* - West Bay Al Corniche الكورنيش / الخليج الغربي -: *Opening Hours* - 16:00-00:00 (Friday 13:00-00:00) -: *Cost per person appx* ***** -: *Phone* - +97444853000 -: *Email* - laliga.doha@sheraton.com -: *WebSite* - www.laligalounge-doha.com -: *Description* - Ideal for football & sports fans. Set in the hotel grounds so accessible to visitors. -: *Book reference number* 14104

AL HUBARA RESTAURANT -: *Type of Location* RESTAURANT -: *GPS* 25.318467, 51.535938 -: *Street* - Al Corniche Sheraton -: *Public Transport if available* - Bus 777 Metro Red Line Doha Exhibition & Conference

Centre (DECC) -: *Town / Area* - West Bay Al Corniche الخليج الغربي / الكورنيش -: *Opening Hours* - Breakfast Buffet: 06:00 AM - 11:00 AM Lunch Buffet: 12:00 PM - 15:30 PM Dinner Buffet: 19:00 PM - 23:30 PM Friday Brunch: 12:30 PM -16:00 PM -: **Cost per person appx** ****** -: *Phone* - +97444853000 -: *Email* - F&Breservations.doha@sheraton.com -: *WebSite* - www.alhubararestaurant.com -: *Description* - Well established venue (in slightly dated public lobby) with excellent food and generally good service. -: *Book reference number* 14122

THE PEARL & KATARA

KATARA كتارا -: *Type of Location* LEISURE LOCATION -: **GPS** 25.360802, 51.524900 -: *Street* - off Lusail Expressway -: *Public Transport if available* - Metro Red Line Al Qassar or Katara -: *Town / Area* - Katara كتارا -: *Opening Hours* - 24 Hours -: **Entrance & cost** No Charge -: *Description* - Katara is a modern cultural area with a number of semi-independent cultural hubs. It is intended to create awareness and appreciation of 'every culture and civilisation'. Workshops, events and exhibitions create a dynamic environment. The built environment adds to the appeal, with a planned design and covered walkways allowing use during all the year. The beachfront adds to its appeal, all-be-it pay to enter. Certainly, this is very much worth visiting to experience a modern Arab townscape. -: *Book reference number* 30020

ARAB POSTAL STAMPS MUSEUM متحف الطوابع البريدية العربية -: *Type of Location* MUSEUM -: **GPS** 25.359045, 51.525464 -: *Street* - off Lusail Expressway -: *Public Transport if available* - Metro Red Line Al Qassar -:

Town / Area - Katara كتارا -: *Opening Hours* - 09:00-21:00
Sun-Thurs / 09:00-12:00 17:00-20:00 Sat -: **Entrance &
cost** No Charge -: *Phone* - +974 4409 1107 -: *Email* -
azayan@hotmail.com -: *WebSite* - http://www.katara.net -:
Description - A exhibition covering the Arab world's philat-
elic history. The online ordering service is of interest to
collectors www.qatarpost.qa/webstore/ -: *Book reference
number* 12600

Katara

QATAR PHOTOGRAPHIC SOCIETY الجمعية
القطرية للتصوير الضوئي -: *Type of Location* MUSEUM -:
GPS 25.359783, 51.525079 -: *Street* - off Lusail
Expressway -: *Public Transport if available* - Metro Red
Line Al Qassar or Katara -: *Town / Area* - Katara كتارا -:
Opening Hours - 08:00-13:00 / 17:00-21:00 with varia-
tions for events. -: **Entrance & cost** No Charge -: *Phone* -
0097444081812 -: *Email* - qps2628k@gmail.com -:
WebSite - www.qpsphoto.qa -: *Description* - The Qatar
Photographic Society hold exhibitions, along with lectures,
workshops and competitions to encourage the art of photog-

raphy in Doha. Shops selling camera equipment abound in Doha; however, spare parts and accessories are more limited and may be expensive. Worth dropping into during a visit into Katara. -: *Book reference number* 12612

KAC (KATARA ART CENTRE) مركز كتارا للفنون -: *Type of Location* MUSEUM CULTURE -: ***GPS*** 25.360622, 51.527597 -: *Street* - east of Lusail Expressway -: *Public Transport if available* - Metro Red Line Al Qassar or Katara -: *Town / Area* - Katara كتارا -: *Opening Hours* - Sat-Thurs 10:00-22:00 Friday 14:00-22:00 (departments do work shorter hours) -: ***Entrance & cost*** No Charge -: *Phone* - +974 4408 0244 -: *Email* - hello@dohakac.com -: *WebSite* - www.dohakac.com -: *Description* - An art gallery, workshop, artists 'incubator', retail outlet for art and interior design. This, like so many art centres and museums in Doha, is decidedly modern in outlook. Its location in Katara adds to its appeal. -: *Book reference number* 12620

KATARA PIGEON TOWERS كتار - برج الحمام -: *Type of Location* SCULPTURE -: ***GPS*** 25.359202, 51.524971 -: *Street* - off Lusail Expressway -: *Public Transport if available* - Metro Red Line Al Qassar -: *Town / Area* - Katara كتارا -: *Opening Hours* - 24 Hours -: *Description* - Three ornate Pigeon Towers. These towers take their inspiration from pigeon towers much of the greater 'Fertile Crescent of antiquity, most especially for this design those of the Nile Delta. Those antique towers are specifically built to house pigeons so that their guano can be collected as soil fertiliser or supply of birds for pigeon pie. Iranian towers may incorporate a wind tower design to cool the interior. These Doha ones with their white doves are ornamental rather than as used originally. Next to them is a Persian style tiled mosque, with exterior ablution block. -: *Book reference number* 15006

Pigeon towers Katara

THE FORCE OF NATURE الطبيعة قوة - تمثال -:
Type of Location SCULPTURE -: ***GPS*** 25.359943, 51.527043 -: *Street* - Katara Amphitheatre -: *Public Transport if available* - Metro Red Line Al Qassar or Katara -: *Town / Area* - Katara كتارا -: *Opening Hours* - 24 Hours -: *Description* - This statue by Italian artist Lorenzo Quinn, is exactly what it says, a tribute to the force of nature, made of bronze, iron and stainless steel. Similar statues to this Katara one can be seen elsewhere

including in Berkley Square London. -: *Book reference number* 15018

THREE MONKEYS -: *Type of Location* SCULPTURE -: *GPS* 25.359320, 51.526570 -: *Street* - Katara Amphitheatre -: *Public Transport if available* - Metro Red Line Al Qassar or Katara -: *Town / Area* - Katara كتارا -: *Opening Hours* - 24 Hours -: *Description* - Gandhi's Three Monkeys by Subodh Gupta based on 'see no evil, hear no evil, speak no evil' are just outside Saffron Lounge restaurant in Katara. -: *Book reference number* 15024

AL GANNAS القناص -: *Type of Location* LEISURE CULTURE -: *GPS* 25.362383, 51.526587 -: *Street* - off Lusail Expressway -: *Public Transport if available* - Metro Red Line Al Qassar or Katara -: *Town / Area* - Katara كتارا -: *Opening Hours* - 07:00-14:00 -: ***Entrance & cost*** No Charge -: *Phone* - 974-44081366 -: *Email* - algannasqtr@katara.net -: *WebSite* - www.algannas.net -: *Description* - Al Gannas (The Hunter) is an organisation which promotes the tradition of Falconry or Saluki hunting. Their headquarters in Katara is in the shape of a Falcons 'Burka' (Rufter). They hold an annual festival during most of January in the sand desert south-west of Mesaieed (very appx location 24.894087, 51.465177) with Falcon hunting and Saluki races. Free 4x4 transport is provided from the 'Sealine Roundabout' 24.863133, 51.513721. For this event it is essential to check with organisers and ideally take their complimentary transport offer. This is very much a worthwhile even to attend. -: *Book reference number* 12502

KATARA MULTI-PURPOSE CENTRE مركز كتارا متعدد الأغراض -: *Type of Location* LEISURE LOCATION -: *GPS* 25.360421, 51.525851 -: *Street* - off Lusail Expressway -: *Public Transport if available* - Metro Red

Line Al Qassar or Katara -: *Town / Area* - Katara كتارا -:
Opening Hours - as per events -: **Entrance & cost** -:
Phone - +97444080050 -: -: *Email* - events@katara.net -:
WebSite –www.katara.net/en/katara-halls -: *Description* -
A modern multi-purpose function centre, for events, exhibi-
tions, meetings and even weddings. On its 'roof' is an
Amphitheatre with 5,000 seats that has held a variety of
performances. Check media for upcoming events here. -:
Book reference number 30022

Beach at Katara

OPERA HOUSE دار الأوبرا -: *Type of Location*
LEISURE LOCATION -: **GPS** 25.359664, 51.524723 -:
Street - Lusail Expressway -: *Public Transport if available* -
Metro Red Line Al Qassar or Katara -: *Town / Area* -
Katara كتارا -: *Opening Hours* - as per performance -:
Entrance & cost Per Event -: *Phone* - +974 4454 8185 -:
Email - events@katara.net -: *WebSite* - www.katara.net -:
Description - Surprisingly for Qatar this is a traditional
looking Opera House. The first performance was held in

December 2010 Performances are principally during the winter and include both classical western and other cultures performances. The building is the home for the Qatar Philharmonic Orchestra www.qatarphilharmonicorchestra.org which held its first performance in October 2008. As with so much in Qatar, the orchestra's performances are focused on the new. They support rising new Arab performers and composers with performances both in Qatar and worldwide. -: *Book reference number* 30028

DOHA FILM INSTITUTE -: *Type of Location* LEISURE -: ***GPS*** 25.358937, 51.525818 -: *Street* - off Lusail Expressway -: *Public Transport if available* - Metro Red Line Al Qassar -: *Town / Area* - Katara كتارا -: *Opening Hours* - 08:00-16:00 -: ***Entrance & cost*** per film -: *Phone* - +974 4420 0505 -: *Email* - info@dohafilminstitute.com -: *WebSite* - www.dohafilminstitute.com -: *Description* - Doha Film Institute funds and supports production of local, regional and international films with an Arab focus. It hosts film screenings (check local media or web site - most are at the weekend), educational programmes and workshops. -: *Book reference number* 12002

KATARA BEACH CLUB -: *Type of Location* LEISURE -: ***GPS*** 25.360979, 51.529205 -: *Street* - off Shakespeare St -: *Public Transport if available* - Metro Red Line Katara -: *Town / Area* - Katara كتارا -: *Opening Hours* - 06:00-22:00 -: ***Entrance & cost*** per choice -: *Phone* - +974 4408 1580 -: *Email* - reception@katarabeachclub.com -: *WebSite* - www.katarabeachclub.com -: *Description* - An upmarket Spa & Gym directly on the beach at Katara -: *Book reference number* 12007

WATER TAXI العبارة -: *Type of Location* LEISURE ACTIVITY -: ***GPS*** 25.364886, 51.540731 -: *Street* - Porto

Arabia Avenue -: *Public Transport if available* - No public transport -: *Town / Area* - The Pearl اللولو -: *Opening Hours* - 14:00-00:00 (Public service) -: **Entrance & cost** QR25/- -: *Phone* - +974 4409 5279 -: *Email* - hmo@ronauticame.com -: *WebSite* - www.ronauticame.com -: *Description* - Within The Pearl this public 'water taxi' operates around the enclosed bay area for 20minutes. It's almost quicker to walk, however as a holiday activity in Doha this is a good hour or so of enjoyment. There are several gates - between GPS25.364886, 51.540731 (organise tickets here) & GPS25.366375, 51.545409. Private hire is possible, against advance booking and charge QR200/- . A longer trip that includes the 'Qanat Quarter' (reminiscent of Venice) to The Pearl's north has a charge of QR50/- for around 40minutes. -: *Book reference number* 12022

CARBON WHEELS -: *Type of Location* LEISURE ACTIVITY -: **GPS** 25.376061, 51.545442 -: *Street* - Off Pearl Boulevard (near Rialto Bridge) -: *Public Transport if available* - No public transport on publication date - expect this to change close to 2022 -: *Town / Area* - The Pearl اللولو -: *Opening Hours* - 12:00-21:00 -: **Entrance & cost** bikes available for sales -: *Phone* - +974 4441 9048 -: *Email* - info@carbonwheels.qa -: *WebSite* - www.carbonwheels.qa -: *Description* - Bike sale and service -: *Book reference number* 12008

LAGOONA MALL -: *Type of Location* SHOPPING MALL -: **GPS** 25.375962, 51.525307 -: *Street* - Off Lusail Highway -: *Public Transport if available* - No public transport -: *Town / Area* - The Pearl اللولو -: *Opening Hours* - 10:00-22:00 (Fri 14:00-12:00) -: *Phone* - +974 4433 5555 -: *Email* - Lagoona@darwishholding.com -: *WebSite* - www.lagoonamall.com/ -: *Description* - a few major 5* hotels medium to high price mall with 'Fifty One East' a major Qatari department store with branches elsewhere in Doha, banks, fashion. Slightly out of the way so not a busy as other malls -: *Book reference number* 20004

DOHA GOLF CLUB نادي الدوحة للغولف -: *Type of Location* SPORT FACILITY -: ***GPS*** 25.380124, 51.505047 -: *Street* - off Al Jamia St -: *Public Transport if available* - Bus 102X Metro Red Line Qatar University (a short taxi ride) -: *Town / Area* - West Bay الخليج الغربي -: *Opening Hours* - 06:00-21:00 -: ***Entrance & cost*** Per event -: *Phone* - +974 4496 0777 -: *Email* - info@dohagolf-club.com -: *WebSite* - www.dohagolfclub.com -: *Description* - Popular well established 72par 18 hole course holds the Qatar Masters in March, -: *Book reference number* 22010

L'WZAAR SEAFOOD -: *Type of Location* RESTAURANT -: ***GPS*** 25.358300, 51.526362 -: *Street* - off Al Moasses St/Lusail Highway -: *Public Transport if available* - Metro Red Line Al Qassar -: *Town / Area* - Katara كتارا -: *Opening Hours* - 12:00 16:00 - 19:00-23:30 (Friday 13:00 16:00 - 19:00-23:30) -: ***Cost per person appx*** **** -: *Phone* - +974 4408 0710 -: *Email* - info@lwzaar.com -: *WebSite* - www.lwzaar.com/ -: *Description* - Seafront seafood restaurant, what's not to like? From sushi to fish & chips, there is a complete range of sea-food overlooking the sea. In cooler weather, choose outdoor, especially in the afternoon when the sun drops behind the building. Ask for window seats -: *Book reference number* 14076

SUKAR PASHA خيام سكرباشا -: *Type of Location* RESTAURANT -: ***GPS*** 25.357267, 51.526520 -: *Street* - off Lusail Expressway -: *Public Transport if available* - Metro Red Line Al Qassar -: *Town / Area* - Katara كتارا -:

Opening Hours - Fri 08:00-11:00/12:30-01:00 -: **Cost per person appx** **** -: *Phone* - +974 4408 2000 -: *Email* - info@sukarpasha.qa. -: *WebSite* - http://sukarpasha.qa -: *Description* - Turkish restaurant set directly on an extension on the Katara beach. Elegant interior, interior and exterior tables - overlooking the sea. Indoor dining or in less humid weather choose outdoor. The location is difficult to beat; however, the service and quality of food are patchy at a premium price. -: *Book reference number* 14086

SAFFRON LOUNGE -: *Type of Location* RESTAU-RANT -: **GPS** 25.359269, 51.526414 -: *Street* - off Lusail Express (adjacent to Katara Hall) -: *Public Transport if available* - Metro Red Line Al Qassar or Katara -: *Town / Area* - Katara كتارا -: *Opening Hours* - 12:00-22:00 (Friday 13:00-23:00) -: **Cost per person appx** ***** -: *Phone* - +974 4408 0808 -: *Description* - Elegant surroundings and good north Indian food. -: *Book reference number* 14110

ALISON NELSON'S CHOCOLATE BAR - CHAIN -: *Type of Location* RESTAURANT -: **GPS** 25.365801, 51.540701 -: *Street* - Porto Arabia Drive -: *Public Transport if available* - No public transport -: *Town / Area* - The Pearl اللولو -: *Opening Hours* - 08:00-01:00 -: **Cost per person appx** ** -: *Phone* - +974 4040 3944 -: *Email* - marketing@hdc-global.com -: *WebSite* - http://www.hdc-www.global.com/restaurants/chocolate-bar.aspx -: *Description* - Light meals from pancakes to pasta - and yes, chocolate desserts, don't miss the innovative fresh juices. Indoor or outdoor seating - it might not be Leonidas chocolate, but worth a detour. -: *Book reference number* 14030

LAYALI IN LAGOONA MALL -: *Type of Location* RESTAURANT -: **GPS** 25.377151, 51.525832 -: *Street* -

off Pearl Boulevard -: *Public Transport if available* - No public transport -: *Town / Area* - The Pearl اللولو -: *Opening Hours* - 09:00-23:30 -: **Cost per person appx** *** -: *Phone* - +974 44310005 -: *Email* - layali@adaragroup.co -: *WebSite* - www.layalirestaurantqatar.com/ -: *Description* - Reasonable Lebanese restaurant, a good medium cost choice in an expensive area. -: *Book reference number* 14054

SHAKESPEARE AND CO = CHAIN -: *Type of Location* RESTAURANT -: **GPS** 25.373242, 51.543407 -: *Street* - Port Arabia Drive -: *Public Transport if available* - No public transport -: *Town / Area* - The Pearl اللولو -: *Opening Hours* - 08:00-23:30 -: **Cost per person appx** *** -: *Phone* - +974 6629 3821 -: *Email* - corporate@shakespeareandco.ae -: *WebSite* - www.shakespeare-and-co.com -: *Description* - An Edwardian, Louis XVI fusion theme for Instagram with international light meals. Overlooking the marina in The Pearl, an Emirati owned chain. -: *Book reference number* 14058

AL SUFRA -: *Type of Location* RESTAURANT -: **GPS** 25.375987, 51.549105 -: *Street* - Marsa Malaz Kempinski, Pearl Boulevard -: *Public Transport if available* - No public transport -: *Town / Area* - The Pearl اللولو -: *Opening Hours* - 12:30-00:00 -: **Cost per person appx** ***** -: *Phone* - +974 4035 5011 -: *Email* - restaurants.marsamalaz@kempinski.com -: *WebSite* - https://www.kempinski.com/en/doha/marsa-malaz-kempinski-the-pearl-doha/dining/restaurants/al-sufra/ -: *Description* - Uniformly excellent food, wine, service and attractive, subdued Arabic inspired ambience. -: *Book reference number* 14092

BURJ AL HAMAM -: *Type of Location* RESTAU-

RANT -: **GPS** 25.365988, 51.540769 -: *Street* - Porto Arabia Drive -: *Public Transport if available* - No public transport -: *Town / Area* - The Pearl اللولو -: *Opening Hours* - 08:00-00:00 (Friday closed 11:30-12:30) -: **Cost per person appx** ***** -: *Phone* - +974 3325 9205 -: *Email* - burjalhamam@hdc-global.com   -:   *WebSite*   - http://www.hdc-global.com/restaurants/burjal-hamam.aspx -: *Description* - A branch of an acclaimed well established Beirut restaurant. -: *Book reference number* 14100

MORIMOTO (MONDRIAN DOHA) -: *Type of Location* RESTAURANT -: **GPS** 25.377467, 51.523363 -: *Street* - Pearl Boulevard/ Lusail Expressway -: *Public Transport if available* - No public transport -: *Town / Area* - The Pearl اللولو -: *Opening Hours* - 18:00-23:30 (Closed Sunday) -: **Cost per person appx** ****** -: *Phone* - +974 4045 5999 -: *Email* - Wineanddine-mondriandoha@sbe.com -: *WebSite* - www.morganshotelgroup.com/mondrian/mondrian-doha/ -: *Description* - Stylish restaurant with food and service commensurate with cost. -: *Book reference number* 14144

NOZOMI (MARSA MALAZ KEMPINSKI) -: *Type of Location* RESTAURANT -: **GPS** 25.377185, 51.549348 -: *Street* - Pearl Boulevard/ Lusail Expressway -: *Public Transport if available* - No public transport -: *Town / Area* - The Pearl اللولو -: *Opening Hours* - 19:00-23:00 (Thurs & Friday also 12:00-15:30) -: **Cost per person appx** ****** -: *Phone* - +974 4035 5089 -: *Email* - info@nozomidoha.com -: *WebSite* - http://www.nozomi-doha.com/ -: *Description* - A view over the man-made lagoon around Marsa Malaz Kempinski. This is a premium restaurant in a premium hotel within which you should expect and will

usually get superlative service. -: *Book reference number* 14148

TORO TORO (MARSA MALAZ KEMPINSKI)

-: *Type of Location* RESTAURANT -: ***GPS*** 25.377356, 51.549124 -: *Street* - The Pearl Boulevard -: *Public Transport if available* - No public transport -: *Town / Area* - The Pearl اللؤلؤ -: *Opening Hours* - 19:00-01:00 (Friday 19:00-02:00) -: ***Cost per person appx*** ****** -: *Phone* - +974 4035 5101 -: *Email* - contact form -: *WebSite* - www.toro-torodoha.com -: *Description* - Overlooking the lagoon of Marsa Malaz Kempinski, Latin American themed restaurant with good food and patchy service -: *Book reference number* 14164

AL WAKRAH, MESAIEED & SOUTH QATAR

QATAR RACING CLUB نادي سباق قطر -: *Type of Location* LEISURE ACTIVITY -: ***GPS*** 25.174843, 51.480552 -: *Street* - north of G Ring Road -: *Public Transport if available* - Bus 20, 32 -: *Town / Area* - Khor Al Udaid / Mesaieed خور العديد / مسيعيد -: *Opening Hours* - as per schedule -: ***Entrance & cost*** per event -: *Phone* - +974-40286000 -: *WebSite* - www.qrc.qa -: *Description* - A track for Motor Bike and Car racing & timed circuits. Events are held mainly Thursday/Friday/Saturday from 18:00 during winter October-April. On main race days it's a good opportunity to see 'muscle cars' shown off. -: *Book reference number* 12018

GULF YOUTH BICYCLE -: *Type of Location* LEISURE ACTIVITY -: ***GPS*** 25.214322, 51.579642 -: *Street* - off Al Wakrah Rd -: *Public Transport if available* -

Bus 10, 109, 119, 129 Metro Red Line Ras Abu Fontas -: *Town / Area* - Barwa Village قرية بروة -: *Opening Hours* - 08:00-12:30-16:00-22:00 (Friday 16:00-22:00) -: ***Entrance & cost*** bikes available for sale -: *Phone* - +974 4455 1092 -: *Description* - Sell bikes, mainly cheap aimed at children but usually a few adults in stock -: *Book reference number* 12012

AL WAKRAH SOUQ الوكرة -: *Type of Location* CULTURAL-: ***GPS*** 25.172235, 51.611205 -: *Street* - west of Al Wakrah Main St, 19km drive south of Doha. -: *Public Transport if available* - Bus 109, 119, 129 Metro Al Wakrah Red Line -: *Town / Area* - Al Wakrah الوكرة -: *Opening Hours* - 24hours *Description* - comparable to Souq Waqif, a mix of shops, places to eat and small hotels. An attractive sea front location adds to the appeal. To the south is a small fishing harbour. There is usually plenty of car parking space. To the west across the main road is a substantial private fort GPS25.172414, 51.605611, this is not open. -: *Book reference number* 10008

JEBEL NAKHSH جبل نخش -: *Type of Location* PUBLIC SPACE -: ***GPS*** 24.875118, 50.907424 -: *Street* - West of the Salwa Rd near the Saudi Arabian border. -: *Public Transport if available* - No public transport -: *Town / Area* - Salwa سلوى -: *Opening Hours* - 24 Hours -: ***Cost per person appx*** No charge -: *Description* - One of the more distinctive hills in Qatar, due to it rising sharply about 100metres above the surrounding plain. Remains of fossil sea creatures from the Miocene period can be seen embedded in the rock. The site is 1km off the road; a long walk is possible if a 4x4 is not available. -: *Book reference number* 12652

CAMEL & FALCON ACTIVITIES أنشطة الجمال

والصقور -: *Type of Location* LEISURE CULTURE -: ***GPS*** 24.862205, 51.512172 -: *Street* - Sealine Beach Rd -: *Public Transport if available* - No public transport -: *Town / Area* - Khor Al Udaid / Mesaieed مسيعيد / خور العديد -: *Opening Hours* - appx 07:00-19:00 -: ***Entrance & cost*** No Charge -: *Phone* - -: *Description* - Here and a bit south along the road near the Sealine Hotel are casual Camel Rides and usually Falcon handlers, negotiate the charge. -: *Book reference number* 12508

Driving down the dunes Khor Al Udaid

KHOR AL UDAID خور العديد (Khor is sometimes spelt Khawr)-: *Type of Location* PUBLIC SPACE -: ***GPS*** 24.635258, 51.389961 -: *Street* - South of Mesaieed -: *Public Transport if available* - No public transport -: *Town / Area* - Khor Al Udaid خور العديد -: *Opening Hours* - 24 Hours -: ***Cost per person appx*** No charge -: *Description* - Dramatic dune and seascape. If you can find undisturbed *sabkha* here, and elsewhere, look for the gypsum crystal formation called a 'Desert Rose'. This small formation, usually a few centimetres, is caused by the evaporated deposits of gypsum or barite (sulphates) which include some sand. This desert rose formation inspired the National Museum's architecture. The steeper dune slopes here, most especially undisturbed isolated barchan dunes, become 'singing sands' when the slope collapses and the vibration of the sand grains passing themselves causes an audible and physical vibration to the dune. This is not a completely empty landscape; small tourist camps near the beach have meals available. One of the more visited locations in Qatar. Less than 100km from central Doha and less than two hours drive, this is relatively easy to get to with capable drivers and 4x4 vehicle (travel with more than one car). Care needs to be taken as the southern sections are Saudi Arabian territory - the border is mid lagoon less than 200meters from the dunes. -: *Book reference number* 12654

GULF ADVENTURES CAMP BEACH CAMP - : *Type of Location* LEISURE -: ***GPS*** 24.804555, 51.490591 -: *Street* - On the East Coast south of Mesaieed مسيعيد -: *Public Transport if available* - No public transport -: *Town / Area* - Khor Al Udaid / Mesaieed خور / مسيعيد العديد -: *Opening Hours* - 24 hours -: ***Entrance & cost*** per film -: *Phone* - +974 4436 1461 -: *WebSite* - www.gulf-adventures.com -: *Description* - This private camp run by Gulf Adventures offers a getaway from Doha - ideal if you don't like self-catering camping. -: *Book reference number* 12004

Desert camp

MAS'HABIYA AND AL ORAIQ محميه لعريق
المسحبيه -: *Type of Location* PUBLIC SPACE -: **GPS**
24.836703, 50.875624 -: *Street* - east of Junction 5 on the
Salwa Rd close to Salwa Beach -: *Public Transport if available* - No public transport -: *Town / Area* - Salwa سلوى -:
Opening Hours - 24 Hours -: **Entrance & cost** No
charge -: *Description* - This is a protect area of gravel plain,
sand sheets, wadis, mesa, etc. The vegetation consists of
*Acacia tortilis, A. ehrenbergiana, Lycium shawii, Ziziphus
spina christi,* etc. is a fenced breeding facility for the previously native ungulates, sand gazelle and Arabian oryx, and
ostrich also Arabian hare, a large number of bird species,

spiny-tailed lizard, etc include the fauna. This reserve is visited by appointment. -: *Book reference number* 12656

AL WAKRAH (Al Janoub) STADIUM -: *Type of Location* SPORT 2022 -: ***GPS*** 25.159483, 51.575420 -: *Street* - Khat Al Wakrah Rd -: *Public Transport if available* - Bus 119 -: *Town / Area* - Al Wakrah الوكرة -: *Opening Hours* - As per event -: *Description* - A stadium for the 2022 World Cup designed by the late Zahra Hadid & AECOM 40,000 seats. Its opening took place in May 2019 -: *Book reference number* 21006

MESAIEED GOLF CLUB نادي مسييعيد للغولف -: *Type of Location* SPORT FACILITY -: ***GPS*** 24.983724, 51.543104 -: *Street* - Mesaieed City Rd -: *Public Transport if available* - Bus 109 -: *Town / Area* - Khor Al Udaid / Mesaieed خور العديد / مسييعيد -: *Opening Hours* - 07:00-22:00 -: ***Entrance & cost*** Per event -: *Phone* - +974 4477 1740 -: *Email* - phone contact -: *WebSite* - http://qpic.qa/MesaieedGolfClub/Pages/Home.aspx -: *Description* - Less developed course, though it is the original course in Doha and still has some 'brown' greens and is part of the oil company's facilities. Also available are a swimming pool and tennis. -: *Book reference number* 22014

BHARATH VASANTHA BHAVAN CHAIN OF 4 -: *Type of Location* RESTAURANT -: ***GPS*** 25.172024, 51.597887 -: *Street* - AbdulRahman bin Jassim St / Ras Abu Abboud -: *Public Transport if available* - Bus 109, 119, 109 / Metro Gold Line National Museum -: *Town / Area* - Al Wakrah الوكرة -: *Opening Hours* - 07:00–15:00 06:00–23:00 (Closed 11:00-12:30 Friday) -: ***Cost per person appx*** ** -: *Phone* - +974 44439955 -: *Description* - Vegan and vegetarian restaurant, South Indian style (spicy) -: *Book reference number* 14036

ZAMAN AL KHAIR RESTAURANT -: *Type of Location* RESTAURANT -: ***GPS*** 25.185942, 51.599628 - : *Street* - Al Wakrah Main St -: *Public Transport if available* - Bus109,119,129 -: *Town / Area* - Al Wakrah الوكرة -: *Opening Hours* - 08:00-00:00 -: ***Cost per person appx*** **** -: *Phone* - +974 4498 6111 -: *Email* - info@zamanalkhairrest.com -: *WebSite* - www.zamanalkhairrest.com -: *Description* - On route to Khor Al Udaid - a choice of dine-in or takeaway. -: *Book reference number* 14090

MERCATO ANTICO (ALSO BRANCH IN TAWAR MALL) -: *Type of Location* RESTAURANT -: ***GPS*** 25.172042, 51.611091 -: *Street* - off Al Wakrah Main St -: *Public Transport if available* - Bus 129 -: *Town / Area* - Al Wakrah الوكرة -: *Opening Hours* - 16:00-00:00 (Friday & Saturday 13:00-00:00) -: ***Cost per person appx*** ****** - : *Phone* - +974 4441 0020 -: *Email* - info@mercato-antico.com -: *WebSite* - www.mercato-antico.com/en/ -: *Description* - Overlooking beach a sepia-toned interior looks out over blue sea and sky. Premium priced food and good service make it largely worth the visit. -: *Book reference number* 14142

NORTH-EAST

VOX CINEMA -: *Type of Location* LEISURE -: ***GPS*** 25.386453, 51.443495 -: *Street* - Junction Al Shamal Rd -: *Public Transport if available* - Bus 170, -: *Town / Area* - Al Daayen الضعاين -: *Opening Hours* - check film schedule -: ***Entrance & cost*** per film -: https://qat.voxcinemas.com/contact-us -: *WebSite* - qat.voxcinemas.com -: *Description* - Multiplex cinema with 3D. Films are censored in Qatar, which may affect how you understand the plot. -: *Book reference number* 12006

THE CHALLENGE 2015 -: *Type of Location* SCULPTURE -: ***GPS*** 25.482525, 51.462959 -: *Street* - Lusail Multipurpose Hall off Al Khor Rd -: *Public Transport if available* - No public transport -: *Town / Area* - Lusail (Losail) لوسيل -: *Opening Hours* - 24 Hours -: *Description* - The Challenge 2015 by Ahmed al-Bahrani are 5 giant hands reaching for a basketball outside the Lusail Multipurpose Hall -: *Book reference number* 15016

Losail Racing Circuit Club

LOSAIL RACING CIRCUIT CLUB حلبة الوسيل للسباقات -: *Type of Location* LEISURE LOCATION -: ***GPS*** 25.487635, 51.448507 -: *Street* - Al Khor Coastal Rd -: *Public Transport if available* - No public transport on publication date - expect this to change close to 2022 -: *Town / Area* - Lusail (Losail) لوسيل -: *Opening Hours* - 24 Hours -: ***Entrance & cost*** per event -: *Phone* - +974 4472 9151 -: *Email* - info@lcsc.qa -: *WebSite* - www.circuitlosail.com -: *Description* - Motor (car, bike, go-cart) race track (5.3km) with track days at least once a month for each variety. You should check directly with the club for a schedule. Various dining and hospitality options are available. -: *Book reference number* 30024

DOHA FESTIVAL CITY دوحة فيستيفال ستي -: *Type of Location* SHOPPING MALL -: *GPS* 25.386453, 51.443495 -: *Street* - Junction Al Shamal Rd (Route 1)and -: *Public Transport if available* - Bus 170, -: *Town / Area* - Al Daayen الضعاين -: *Opening Hours* - 10:00-22:00 (Friday closed 11:30-13:00) -: *Phone* - +974 4035 4444 -: *Email* - info@dohafestivalcity.com -: *WebSite* - www.dohafestivalcity.com -: *Description* - Large shopping mall, with indoor snow toboggan slope. Mid-price retail outlets including IKEA, Riva, Next, Debenhams, Old Navy and a large range of restaurants. Similar to shopping malls the world over, this is 18km north of Doha centre, so it might be a stretch to visit though it's probably the most complete shopping option in Doha. -: *Book reference number* 20002

AL BAYT STADIUM -: *Type of Location* SPORT 2022 -: *GPS* 25.652193, 51.484363 -: *Street* - Al Khor Coastal Rd -: *Public Transport if available* - Bus 102 -: *Town / Area* - Al Khor الخور -: *Opening Hours* - As per event -: *Description* - A stadium for the 2022 World Cup designed to look like an Arab tent with 60,000 seats expected to open in 2019 -: *Book reference number* 21000

LUSAIL MULTIPURPOSE SPORTS ARENA ملعب لوسيل الرياضي -: *Type of Location* SPORT 2022 -: *GPS* 25.481884, 51.461916 -: *Street* - Al Khor Coastal Rd -: *Public Transport if available* - No public transport on publication date - expect this to change close to 2022 -: *Town / Area* - Lusail (Losail) لوسيل -: *Opening Hours* - As per event -: -: *Phone* - +974 4494 4777 -: *Email* - qoc@olympic.qa -: *WebSite* - www.olympic.qa -: *Description* - A substantial multi-use indoor sports arena. Indoor football, basketball, squash and other sports. South of this arena is the Qatar shooting and archery complex www.qatarshooting.qa. -: *Book reference number* 21012

LUSAIL STADIUM -: *Type of Location* SPORT 2022 -: *GPS* 25.421058, 51.491833 -: *Street* - Al Khor Coastal Rd -: *Public Transport if available* - No public transport on publication date - expect this to change close to 2022 -: *Town / Area* - Lusail (also spelt Losail) لوسيل -: *Opening Hours* - As per event -: *Description* - A stadium for the 2022 World Cup with 80,000 seats to open in 2021 -: *Book reference number* 21014

BARZAN TOWERS ابراج برزان -: *Type of Location* HISTORICAL -: *GPS* 25.418353, 51.413210 -: *Street* - 6km drive from the Al Khiraitiyat Interchange on Al Shamal Rd (Route 1)(Doha Expressway) about 23km north-west of Al Corniche -: *Public Transport if available* - Bus 102 (1200metres) -: *Town / Area* - Umm Salal أم صلال -: *Opening Hours* - casual visit -: *Entrance & cost* No charge -: *Description* - A couple of interesting fortified towers in a small park, north of Doha centre. They were built in the early 20thc by Sheikh Mohammed bin Jassim Al Thani. Though restored the impact is authentic, including resident pigeons! -: *Book reference number* 10014

AL DAKHERA / AL DAKHIRA / AL THAKHIRA الذخيره -: *Type of Location* PUBLIC SPACE -: *GPS* 25.739410, 51.548328 -: *Street* - Al Dakhira -: *Public Transport if available* - Bus 102 -: *Town / Area* - Al Khor الخور -: *Opening Hours* - 24 hours -: ***Entrance & cost*** No charge -: *Description* - This is the largest area of mangrove in Qatar and also has coral reefs, seagrass beds, etc with offshore Hawksbill turtle. Flora includes mangrove *Avicennia marina, Anabis setifera, Salsola imbricate, Lycium shawii,* etc are the dominant plant species. The fauna includes over 130 species of birds, and reptiles including hooded malpolon, spiny-tailed lizard and 44 species of terrestrial insects. Far from a must see on a short visit, but certainly worth including especially if you can organise a boat excursion. -: *Book reference number* 12626

AL KHOR BEACH شاطئ الخور -: *Type of Location* PUBLIC SPACE -: *GPS* 25.716655, 51.593373 -: *Street* - off Al Khor Coastal Rd -: *Public Transport if available* - No public transport -: *Town / Area* - Al Khor الخور -: *Opening Hours* - 24 Hours -: ***Entrance & cost*** No charge -: *Description* - East of Al Khor (after a rough unmarked drive of 4km from a track at 25.708309, 51.553589) is a beach with no lifeguard, safety equipment or facilities. -: *Book reference number* 12628

AL KHOR PARK منتزة الخور -: *Type of Location* PUBLIC SPACE -: *GPS* 25.649055, 51.419751 -: *Street* - Al Shamal Rd (Route 1)-: *Public Transport if available* - Bus 102, 727 or 100,101, -: *Town / Area* - Al Khor الخور -: *Opening Hours* - 08:00-22:00 -: ***Entrance & cost*** QAR5/- -: *Description* - A 20hectar well maintained park. Complete with a miniature railway, small zoo and children's play areas. This offers an alternative to the parks in Doha; the zoo animals would benefit from a more natural environment. -: *Book reference number* 12630

AL EQDA, HORSE OWNERS COMPLEX اسطبلات العقدة -: *Type of Location* LEISURE CULTURE -: *GPS* 25.671835, 51.438386 -: *Street* - off Al Shamal Rd -: *Public Transport if available* - No public transport -: *Town /*

Area - Al Khor الخور -: *Opening Hours* - -: **Entrance & cost** No Charge -: *Phone* - -: *Description* - New private stables, soon to open -: *Book reference number* 12500

PEARL OF BEIRUT RESTAURANT -: *Type of Location* RESTAURANT -: **GPS** 25.685707, 51.514487 -: *Street* - Corniche Al Khor (opposite fish harbour) -: *Public Transport if available* - Bus 102, 102X -: *Town / Area* - Al Khor الخور -: *Opening Hours* - 06:30-23:00 -: **Cost per person appx** * -: *Phone* - +974 4472 0123 -: *Description* - Low cost simple restaurant overlooking sea and dhow harbour (outdoor seating available) . There are other restaurants in the area -: *Book reference number* 14010

TURKIYE KEBAB -: *Type of Location* RESTAURANT -: **GPS** 25.678917, 51.497194 -: *Street* - Al Khor Coastal Rd / Al Khor Town Rd -: *Public Transport if available* - Bus 102, 102X -: *Town / Area* - Al Khor الخور -: *Opening Hours* - 10:00-23:00 -: **Cost per person appx** * -: *Phone* - +974 4411 4150 -: *Description* - Good for take-away and meals in the north of Qatar - main restaurant upstairs. -: *Book reference number* 14022

Al Jassasiya rock art

AL JASSASIYA (AL GASASIA) Rock Art
الجساسية -: Type of Location HISTORICAL -: GPS
25.951881, 51.406147 -: Street - A few kilometres to the
east of route 1 -: Public Transport if available - No public
transport -: Town / Area - Ash Shamal الشمال -: Opening
Hours - casual visit -: Entrance & cost No charge -: Description - This fenced area is promoted by the Qatari government as an area to illustrate Qatar history and maritime
heritage. A gate that might be closed is to the east on the
service road. The site consists of rock art on a low outcrop
of rock. The rock art appears to comprise a series of Dhows
with banks of oars, a number of double rows of sunken
holes that could represent a game. This isolated site, that is
usually possible to enter, is probably of interest to archaeol-
ogists and the like. -: Book reference number 10000

. . .

DUKHAN & WEST COAST, CENTRAL QATAR, AL RUWAIS & NORTH COAST

AL ZUBARAH الآثار الزبارة -: *Type of Location* HISTORICAL -: *GPS* 25.977195, 51.029308 -: *Street* - On the Al Shamal Rd (Route 1)north-west of Doha (about 120km drive) -: *Public Transport if available* - Bus 100 (a 2kilometre walk) -: *Town / Area* - Al Zubarah الزبارة - : *Opening Hours* - casual visit (best made to fit in with fort opening hours) -: *Entrance & cost* No charge -:

Al Zubarah

Description - This is a 60 hectare site of the abandoned town of Al Zubarah. Stretching along a sheltered bay, it offers a partially excavated 200 years old town, an interesting beachfront and sea, and adjacent to them a fort. In winter, there may be archaeological excavations, which may place minor restrictions to where you can walk, but also add immeasurably to the visit if you talk with an archaeologist. For more information, see the UNESCO section. -: *Book reference number* 10012

AL ZUBARAH FORT قلعة الزبارة -: *Type of Location* HISTORICAL -: *GPS* 25.976788, 51.045509 -: *Street* - On the Al Shamal Rd (Route 1) north-west of Doha -: *Public Transport if available* - Bus 100 -: *Town / Area* - Al Zubarah الزبارة -: *Opening Hours* - 07:30-17:00 -: *Entrance & cost* No charge -: *Description* - A small 20th c military fort, built in 1938 as a counter to the fort built by Bahrain on the Hawar Islands. It continued to be used for security purposes until 1986. Currently, it's within a protected area and the UNESCO zone of Al Zubarah. The ground area is about 900sq metres as a square, with on the corners three round towers (with small crenellations) and a square tower, the exterior is lime plastered. A parapet with small rifle-ports rises to protect the wall walk, which itself is made from the roofs of the rooms around the courtyard. A water well occupies part of the open courtyard, and a series of rooms are built around the edge of the courtyard, opening out onto it. Inside a range of photo-descriptions of the area, its history and archaeology. For more information, see the Al Zubarah UNESCO section. Though the fort needs a general refurbishment, it's worth adding on to any visit to the west coast, if only to wonder how such a desolate region could have become a crucial part of Qatar's history. Coupled with the abandoned town of Al Zubarah, this makes an excellent day trip. -: *Book reference number* 10010

Al Zubarah fort

QALAAT AL THAQAB (Al Thaqab Fort) قلعة
الثقب -: *Type of Location* HISTORICAL -: *GPS*
26.032921, 51.117120 -: *Street* - south of Al Ruwais west
of the Coastal Rd & as the Eagle flies 9.5km north-east of
Al Zubarah Fort. -: *Public Transport if available* - No
public transport -: *Town / Area* - Al Ruwais الرويس -:
Opening Hours - casual visit -: *Entrance & cost* No charge -
: *Description* - This small abandoned fort 11km north-east
of Al Zubarah and 14 south-west of Abu Al Dhalouf
village has three towers and a few rooms. It served to
protect the water wells next to the fort. This agricultural
area suffers from lack of water, making the fort obsolete
many years ago. It was restored in 2005 and awaits a
purpose. The style and components are similar to Al
Zubarah Fort, though the exterior is unplastered. The
floral shaped structure next to the fort was built in 2015
presumably as a reference to the wells. Stick to the tracks
leading east off the tarmac road as the soil is like powder

and after rain will trap vehicles, a 4x4 is ideal. This makes an extra stop if visiting Al Zubarah. -: *Book reference number* 10016

UMM AL MAA ام الماء -: *Type of Location* HISTOR-ICAL -: *GPS* 25.817664, 50.991277 -: *Street* - south of Al Shamal Rd, about 93km drive north-west of Doha -: *Public Transport if available* - No public transport -: *Town / Area* - Al Ghuwariyah الغويرية -: *Opening Hours* - casual visit -: *Entrance & cost* No charge -: *Description* - Umm Al Maa 'The Mother of Water' is an area in west Qatar (south of the soon-to-be settlement of Dhbea) with accessible water aquifers and shallow depressions that collect water after rain. About 400 metres from the beach is an area of graves dated variously to the Bronze Age or mid Iron Age. A small late 19thc / early 20th fort is the most noticeable remain. Umm Al Maa is well off any road; a 4x4 is needed. -: *Book reference number* 10020

RAS ABROUQ رأس أبروق -: *Type of Location* PUBLIC SPACE -: *GPS* 25.622260, 50.832476 -: *Street* - North of Dukhan Highway -: *Public Transport if available* - No public transport -: *Town / Area* - Al Jamiliyah الجميلية -: *Opening Hours* - 24 Hours -: ***Entrance & cost*** No charge -: *Description* - In north-west Qatar a peninsula with not only Film City but a remarkable variety of archaeology. Flint-working and scattered stone-age tools might be seen on some of the limestone Mesas. Ubaid pottery of a similar period has been found. The extended coastline of much of west Qatar is at some distance from roads; also note that the Qatar / Bahrain / Saudi international border runs in the sea on the edge of the coastline. The beaches here are over-looked by low limestone cliffs. The most northerly point is a small coastguard station, with the Bahrain waters only a few hundred metres off the beaches. -: *Book reference number* 12658

ZEKREET FORT زكريت قلعة -: *Type of Location* HISTORICAL -: *GPS* 25.490289, 50.844413 -: *Street* - 83km west of Doha off the Dukhan Highway, about 600metres north of the village of Zekreet -: *Public Transport if available* - No public transport -: *Town / Area* - Zekreet زكريت -: *Opening Hours* - casual visit -: *Entrance & cost* No charge -: *Description* - The fort was built around the start of the 19th c. It may have been associated with Rahman ibn Jabir Al Jalahima, (see Al Khuwair). Like Al Zubarah the fort seems to have been abandoned around 1811. The archaeologist Beatrice de Cardi researched the fort in 1974 as part of the Qatar government's initial research into its history. This fort is a simple design of 1,800sqm with three round towers and a square tower, very typical of other Qatari forts; now the walls are only a few layers of stone high. Traces of rooms can be seen against the interior of the walls. Not a very dramatic site, however add this onto visits to the other areas on this south-west coast. One area to note is there are a number of military installations here, so do act sensibly. Also, with the current GCC situation be cautious regarding your proximity to the Hawar Islands of the Bahrain and Saudi borders. -: *Book reference number* 10024

ZEKREET BEACH شاطئ زكريت -: *Type of Location* PUBLIC SPACE -: *GPS* 25.470686, 50.849176 -: *Street* - off Zekreet Rd -: *Public Transport if available* - No public transport -: *Town / Area* - Zekreet زكريت -: *Opening Hours* - 24 Hours -: ***Entrance & cost*** No charge -: *Description* - About 300metres west of the Zekreet Rd this shallow, sheltered lagoon is relatively quiet. Kitesurfing is done here, and the shallow waters are relatively calm. The sand is very loose and a 4x4 is essential and note that as with similarly isolated beaches, there is no lifeguard, safety equipment or facilities. Also, note that the Qatar / Bahrain International Border runs in the sea on the edge of the coastline. -: *Book reference number* 12662

AL REEM BIOSPHERE RESERVE - RAWDAT AL NUMAN منطقة الريم المحمية -: *Type of Location* PUBLIC SPACE -: ***GPS*** 25.860327, 51.080013 -: *Street* - Much of the north-west region of Qatar. There are fenced areas such as Rawdat Al Numan روضة نعمان that included vegetated areas - the word روضة /Rawdha / Rawdat means meadow, which occurs after rain. The area south of film city is also included. -: *Public Transport if available* - No public transport -: *Town / Area* - Ash Shamal الشمال -: *Opening Hours* - 24 Hours -: ***Entrance & cost*** No charge -: *Description* - Covering 1189sq kilometres (Core 605 and Buffer:584) Al Reem covers just over 10% of Qatar's landmass. The overall reserve extends from Al Zubarah on the coast, east to Al Ghuwaitiya and south-west to Zekreet. It is home to limestone cliffs, mesas, wadis, *sabkha*s and gravel plains constitute the terrestrial site. Coastal swampy mudflats, shallow sea waters rich in seagrass beds, land vegetation includes acacia. Ostrich and sand gazelle have been reintroduced. Fauna includes hawksbill and green turtles, dugong, spiny-tailed lizard, Ethiopian hedgehog, red fox and a large number of birds. Sea fauna includes hawksbill and green turtles and dugong. The overall reserve extends from Al Zubarah on the coast, east to Al Ghuwaitiya and south-west to Zekreet. If you are travelling to the west coast, then much of the area is within the reserve. -: *Book reference number* 12634

FILM CITY مدينة السينما -: *Type of Location* LEISURE LOCATION -: ***GPS*** 25.578470, 50.846614 -: *Street* - off route 30 / Dukhan Highway the West Coast Rd taking the track north with your 4x4 from 25.460376, 50.894989 opposite a parking area. The track is about 16km long and do not leave it as the wet areas are *sabkha* where you may get bogged down very quickly. After about 7.4km a track west leads to 4 steel 'planks' about 15m high sunk into the ground, modern art. Close to these (1.5km north-west) is a low cliff face used for rock climbing 25.519947, 50.847781. This track west eventually reaches Zekreet. -: *Public Transport if available* - No public transport -: *Town / Area* - Zekreet زكريت -: *Opening Hours* - 24 Hours -: ***Entrance & cost*** Per film -: Film City a 3,000sqm reimagined Qatari village was created for a Qatari TV series in 2000. It was an inspiration for the renovations of Souq Waqif and Al Wakrah. There is a caretaker who usually welcomes visitors.

Film city

A stone's throw away is a small oasis with roaming ostrich, oryx and gazelle (these are not tame, and therefore care should be taken especially if you have children). A 4x4 is needed as with all off-road tracks - it's vital to have a full petrol tank and at least two vehicles. About a kilometre farther north, on the same route, are several modern stone 'huts' built on a low escarpment and one created on a 'yardang'. These huts are not far from the sea and a few beaches. Note that the northern area of this peninsula is less than a kilometre from Bahrain's territorial waters in which you would be an illegal visitor and beyond the assistance of your embassy. -: *Book reference number* 30016

Yardangs Zekreet

EAST WEST -: *Type of Location* SCULPTURE -: *GPS* 25.517126, 50.870894 -: *Street* - Abrouq nature reserve -: *Public Transport if available* - No public transport -: *Town / Area* - Zekreet زكريت -: *Opening Hours* - 24 Hours -: *Description* - Spread over a distance of 850metres the 4 steel, that are not quite aligned but are named the 'East-West' sculpture. This installation is a big draw in the west of Qatar, created by artist Richard Serra. -: *Book reference number* 15004

DUKHAN BEACH شاطئ دخان -: *Type of Location* PUBLIC SPACE -: *GPS* 25.413912, 50.758946 -: *Street* - Corniche Dukhan -: *Public Transport if available* - Bus 104,104a,137,137a (a walk of 4 kilometres) -: *Town / Area* - Dukhan دخان -: *Opening Hours* - 24 Hours -: ***Entrance & cost*** No charge -: *Description* - Public beach near Dukhan some shelters next to the beach and date palms. Easy access from the tarmac rd. Other stretches of public beach lie along the next few kilometres north and south. -: *Book reference number* 12646

DUKHAN WATER SPORTS CLUB نادي دخان للرياضات المائية -: *Type of Location* LEISURE LOCATION -: *GPS* 25.411153, 50.759644 -: *Street* - off the Dukhan Highway west of Dukhan. -: *Public Transport if available* - A 4kilometre walk (or use a taxi app) from the nearest stop at Dukhan Petrol Station - Bus 104,104a,137,137a (at least every hour). -: *Town / Area* - Dukhan دخان -: *Opening Hours* - 08:00-18:00 -: *Description* - A small well-established club, with access to the sea has many activities including swimming pool and Jet Skies. This is a membership Club for employees of companies associated with Dukhan, if you are in Qatar for some time check with somebody for an entrance pass. -: *Book reference number* 30014

Al RUWAIS BEACH شاطىء الرويس -: *Type of Location* PUBLIC SPACE -: *GPS* 26.144419, 51.215680 -: *Street* - off Al Kasooma St -: *Public Transport if available* - Bus 100, 101, 201 -: *Town / Area* - Al Ruwais الرويس -: *Opening Hours* - 24 Hours -: ***Entrance & cost*** No charge -: *Description* - A small beach, not really for swim-

ming (or sunbathing). Offshore are some traditional intertidal fish traps, 'Maskar' -: *Book reference number* 12636

AL KHUWAIR الخوير -: Type of Location
HISTORICAL -: GPS 26.068476, 51.083353 -: Street -
Off the west coastal Rd -: Public Transport if available - No
public transport -: Town / Area - Al Ruwais الرويس -:
Opening Hours - casual visit -: Entrance & cost No charge -
: Description - This abandoned village was a haunt of
Rahman ibn Jabir Al Jalahima, 'known' as a pirate and the
first to have worn the essential piece of pirate dress an eye
patch. He was previously a partner with the Al Khalifa (of
Bahrain), but feeling he lost out on the benefit of the spoils
of Bahrain became their enemy. He co-operated with the
Al Saud and avoided conflict with Britain, clearly an excellent tactician. Rahman died in battle in 1826. The village
relied on water from the wells at Al Thaqab. The sandbanks and coral off the coast protected the village from
attack. Less than 10km north of Al Khuwair is another
small largely abandoned village Al Jamail (and spelling
variants). Madinat Ash Shamal (and Al Ruwais Port) to the
north of these small placesoffers refreshments, banks and
petrol. Beyond Al Jamail are more abandoned housing
areas and largely undeveloped sandy beaches. Always stay
on tracks as the general area is *sabkha* and soft mud when
wet. These villages are suitable as an add on to Zubarah -:
Book reference number 10002

ISKENDER PASHA -: *Type of Location* RESTAU-
RANT -: **GPS** 26.126788, 51.203828 -: *Street* - off Al
Shamal Rd -: *Public Transport if available* - Bus 101, 201 -:
Town / Area - Al Ruwais الرويس -: *Opening Hours* - 09:00-
23:00 -: **Cost per person appx** * -: *Phone* - +974 3357
4304 -: *Description* - An inexpensive restaurant with Turk-

ish, and Indian, style food. There are several other restaurants (including Tea Time) on the same street, compare these to choose the one that's right for you. -: *Book reference number* 14004

UM TAIS ISLAND جزيرة ام تيس -: *Type of Location* PUBLIC SPACE -: *GPS* 26.156805, 51.276059 -: *Street -* off Al Shamal Rd (Route 1)-: *Public Transport if available -* No public transport -: *Town / Area -* Al Ruwais الرويس -: *Opening Hours -* 24 Hours -: **Entrance & cost** No charge -: *Description -* A substantial sand bar island off Qatar's northern coast. Substantial areas of Mangrove add to its attraction. Opposite, on the mainland, is the only hotel in northern Qatar Zulal Wellness Resort. -: *Book reference number* 12660

JAZIRAT RAS RAKAN (ISLAND) جزيرة ام تيس -: *Type of Location* PUBLIC SPACE -: *GPS* 26.178356, 51.225945 -: *Street -* off Al Shamal Rd (Route 1)-: *Public Transport if available -* No public transport -: *Town / Area -* Al Ruwais الرويس -: *Opening Hours -* 24 Hours -: **Entrance & cost** No charge -: *Description -* A small sandy offshore island with seagrass off its beaches. Opposite, on the mainland, is the only hotel in northern Qatar Zulal Wellness Resort. -: *Book reference number* 12650

AL MAFJAR BEACH شاطئ المفجر -: *Type of Location* PUBLIC SPACE -: *GPS* 26.13579, 51.30072 -: *Street -* off Al Shamal Rd (Route 1)-: *Public Transport if available -* No public transport -: *Town / Area -* Ash Shamal الشمال -: *Opening Hours -* 24 Hours -: **Entrance & cost** No charge -: *Description -* Opposite the small ruined village of Al Mafjar an isolated beach area and sand spit extend to Qatar's most northerly point. The sand is very loose and a 4x4 is essential as with other beaches in Qatar there is no lifeguard, safety equipment or facilities. -: *Book reference number* 12632

FUWAYRIT BEACH شاطئ فويريت -: *Type of Location* PUBLIC SPACE -: *GPS* 26.059074, 51.354279 -: *Street* - East of Al Shamal Rd north of Doha -: *Public Transport if available* - a very long walk of 3 kilometres Bus 101, 201 -: *Town / Area* - Ash Shamal الشمال -: *Opening Hours* - 24 Hours -: **Entrance & cost** No charge -: *Description* - A public beach which is relatively busy at the weekend. Access is via the Al Shamal Rd and then off-road. Camels and sea activities are usually available. Fuwayrit Beach is a crucial location for hawksbill turtle nesting (this beach is closed as a result at peak besting season 1st April to 31 July). To the south of the beach is Al Ghariyah Beach - with slightly more development. -: *Book reference number* 12648

AL WABRA WILDLIFE منطقة حيوان الوبرة -: *Type of Location* PUBLIC SPACE -: *GPS* 25.345738, 51.176107 -: *Street* - south-west of Ash Shahaniyah camel racetrack -: *Public Transport if available* - No public transport -: *Town / Area* - Ash Shahaniyah الشحانية -: *Opening Hours* - by appointment 08:00-18:00 -: **Entrance & cost** No charge -: *Description* - Set up in the mid 1970s as a private zoo and more recently it has developed into a breeding zoo. This needs a bit of organisation to visit but is interesting if you are interested in wildlife. -: *Book reference number* 12638

AL DOSARI ZOO AND GAME RESERVE حديقة ومحمية محمد الدوسري -: *Type of Location* LEISURE LOCATION -: *GPS* 25.440456, 51.224234 -: *Street* - Al Turiyah Rd -: *Public Transport if available* - Bus 104a -: *Town / Area* - Al Shahaniyah الشحانية -: *Opening Hours* - 07:00-19:00 Sat-Friday -: **Entrance & cost** QAR10/- -: *Phone* - +974 44908785 -: *Email* - AlDosariZoo@Hotmail.com -: *Description* - An example of a local private zoo, set up in the manner of a mid-20th century animal display. It will be eclipsed on the re-opening (at an unknown future date) of the Government's Doha Zoo. Additionally there are extra displays and activities with charge including horse and camel rides -: *Book reference number* 30004

SHEIKH FAISAL BIN QASSIM AL THANI MUSEUM متحف الشيخ فيصل بن قاسم آل ثاني -: *Type of Location* MUSEUM -: ***GPS*** 25.350500, 51.261675 -: *Street* - Al Dukhan Highway -: *Public Transport if available* - Bus 104, 104a, 300 -: *Town / Area* - Ash Shahaniyah (near) الشحانية -: *Opening Hours* - Sun-Thurs 09:00-16:00 Fri 14:00-19:00 Sat 10:00-18:00 -: ***Entrance & cost*** No Charge -: *Phone* - -: *Email* - visitors@fbqmuseum.org -: *WebSite* - www.fbqmuseum.org -: *Description* - A eclectic Museum collection created by its eponymous founder; it has Carpets, Classic Cars the Museum and in the adjacent farm animals including Oryx. Entry charge QAR50 (check if the entrance charge includes a photo permit as the policy has changed about this in the past). The collection has no information - so try and organise a guided visit. An interesting place to visit - but it's a way out of Doha. Combine it with the camels at Al Shahaniyah. -: *Book reference number* 12614

CAMEL RACE TRACK ميدان سباق الهجن -: *Type of Location* LEISURE CULTURE -: ***GPS*** 25.402962, 51.205796 -: *Street* - Al Dukhan Highway 39km west of Doha -: *Public Transport if available* - Bus 104, 104a -: *Town / Area* - Ash Shahaniyah الشحانية -: *Opening Hours* - as per events - usually in winter -: ***Entrance & cost*** No Charge -: *Phone* - -: *Description* - - Hidden off the main road races are held at the weekend. There are three tracks inside each other. Camel racing is an important part of Qatari identity as the government promotes it extensively, with not only creating the course but with prizes including the "Golden Sword". Camels themselves often have high value, and all this does create an entire culture around the sport. While in the past the jockey was a small child, today they are robots, remote controlled with a whip to encourage the animal forward along with a walkie-talkie to enable the owner to should instructions from his car that speeds along the track. For the self-respecting camel dozens of cars following each race, with their horns blaring would make them run all day to get away. Races are held at weekends from Oct - Feb - usually in Friday occasionally Saturday as well mornings from 07: 00. However, most morning camels are exercised, so if you are passing, a short stop is worthwhile. What's not to like about camels - and is something unique to the region and quintessentially part of Qatar's culture this is a must see. -: *Book reference number* 12510

MALL OF QATAR -: *Type of Location* SHOPPING MALL -: *GPS* 25.324452, 51.349969 -: *Street* - off Dukhan Highway / National Day Ceremonial Rd -: *Public Transport if available* - Bus 104, 104A from Al Ghanim Bus Station -: *Town / Area* - Al Rayyan الريان -: *Opening Hours* - 10:00-23:00 -: *Phone* - +974 4034 6000 -: *WebSite* - www.mallofqatar.com.qa -: *Description* - far from many other attractions, the Mall of Qatar is on the road to the Camel Race Tracks and west coast. A significant mall, one of the largest in Arabia. Banks, cinema, children's entertainment, Carrefour supermarket, Zara, Salam Stores, Debenhams. With an impressive design and entertainment, this is a destination in itself (despite a good proportion of unoccupied stores) - though with a maze-like access route. As with many other large public areas in Qatar, a subjective entrance policy is in place -: *Book reference number* 20008

AQUA PARK أكوا بارك -: *Type of Location* LEISURE LOCATION -: *GPS* 25.155777, 51.294455 -: *Street* - South of Salwa Rd Rawdath Rashid Interchange -: *Public Transport if available* - no public transport -: *Town / Area* - Abu Nakhla ابو نخلة -: *Opening Hours* - 11:00-20:00 Mon-Weds (Tues Ladies 14:00-22:00) / 10:00-22:00 Thurs-Fri (Fri Family Day) / Sat 10:00-20:00 closed Sunday -: *Entrance & cost* QAR120 entrance / Child QAR100 (plus some rides extra) -: *Phone* - +974 4490 5878 -: *Description* - A relatively large water park, with wave machine, tube slide and more. -: *Book reference number* 30006

AZWAIR FAMILY RESORT منتجع عائلة الزوير -: *Type of Location* LEISURE LOCATION -: *GPS* 25.703686, 50.989948 -: *Street* - west of Al Shamal Rd (Route 1)-: *Public Transport if available* - no public transport 4x4 needed. -: *Town / Area* - near the village of Al Jumayliyah مزرعة ومنتجع الزوير السياحي -: *Opening Hours* - 07:00-19:00 -: *Entrance & cost* QAR15/- -: *Phone* - -: *Description* - A small, isolated, extremely old fashioned location with some caged animals and vehicles. The appeal is minimal, and its isolation makes it well down the list of things to do in Qatar. -: *Book reference number* 30010

MUDHLEM CAVE كهف مظلم -: *Type of Location* LEISURE LOCATION -: *GPS* 25.122699, 51.228117 -: *Street* - South of Salwa Rd Mekainis Interchange -: *Public Transport if available* - No public transport -: *Town / Area* - Mekainis مكينيس -: *Opening Hours* - 24 Hours -: *Entrance & cost* No Charge -: *Description* – south of Musfur Cave, this is a sinkhole with a potentially hazardous scree slope to clamber down to the bottom. Though fenced off many people do gain access -: *Book reference number* 30026

MUSFUR SINKHOLE (Tufail Cave) كهف دحل المصفر -: *Type of Location* LEISURE LOCATION -: ***GPS*** 25.174950, 51.211677 -: *Street* - west of Rawdat Rashed Rd -: *Public Transport if available* - No Public Transport -: *Town / Area* - Mekainis مكينيس -: *Opening Hours* - 24 Hours -: ***Entrance & cost*** No Charge -: *Description* – north of Mudhlem Cave, this is a sinkhole with a potentially hazardous scree slope to clamber down to the bottom. Though fenced off many people do gain access -: *Book reference number* 30025

AL RAYYAN STADIUM -: *Type of Location* SPORT 2022 -: ***GPS*** 25.330051, 51.340853 -: *Street* - Dukhan Highway -: *Public Transport if available* - Bus 104, 104a -: *Town / Area* - Al Rayyan الريان -: *Opening Hours* - As per event -: *Description* - A stadium for the 2022 World Cup with 40,000 seats | Opening: 2021 -: *Book reference number* 21002

CHAPTER TWENTY-NINE

TOUR COMPANIES

BLUE PEARL -: *GPS* 25.368507, 51.547667 -: *Street* - off Lusail Expressway -: *Public Transport if available* - No public transport -: *Area* - The Pearl with activities in several locations across Qatar. اللولو -: *Opening Hours* -random, best to email/phone -: *Phone* - +974666 02 830 -: *Email* - hello@clubbluepearl.com -: *WebSite* - www.bluepearlexperience.com/ -: *Description* - KiteSurf, Standup Paddle, Kayak, Cycling, Camping.

DOHA BUS -: *GPS* 25.267892, 51.494862 -: *Street* - Doha Expresswa/Al Amir St -: *Public Transport if available* - Bus, 31,33a,34,136,136a,137,137a Metro Al Sudan -: *Area* - Al Nasr النصر -: *Opening Hours* - 09:00-18:00 Sat-Wed 09:00-14:00 Thurs - closed Friday -: *Phone* - +97444422444 -: *Email* - hello@dohabus.co -: *WebSite* - www.dohabus.com -: *Description* - Group Bus tours throughout Qatar - a 24 hop-on hop-off type operation - including Souq Waqif.

FALCON TOURS -: *GPS* 25.289378, 51.538962 -: *Street* - Building No : 38 7th floor Abdullah Bin Jassim St,

Doha, Qatar -: *Public Transport if available* - Bus 76, 177 Metro Gold Line Souq Waqif -: *Area* - Souq Waqif سوق واقف -: *Opening Hours* - 08:00-23:00 Sat-Fri -: *Phone* - +974 3144 0129 -: *Email* - info@falcontoursqatar.com -: *WebSite* - www.falcontoursqatar.com -: *Description* - City Tour, Desert Safari, Dhow and Game Fishing, Yacht

GOLDEN ADVENTURES QATAR -: *GPS* 25.267486, 51.544639 -: *Street* - Al Khalidiya Street -: *Public Transport if available* - Bus 11, 757 Metro Umm Ghuwailina -: *Area* - Najma نجمة -: *Opening Hours* - 09:00-20:00 Sat-Fri -: *Phone* - +974 5501 1031 -: *Email* - info@goldenadventuresqatar.com -: *WebSite* - www.goldenadventuresqatar.com -: *Description* - City Tours, Tours to northern & western Qatar, Desert Safari

INBOUND TOURS QATAR -: *GPS* 25.286708, 51.532482 -: *Street* - South of Souq Waqif -: *Public Transport if available* - Bus Al Ghanim Bus Station. Metro Gold-Line Souq Waqif or Red Line Al Doha Al Jadeda. -: *Area* - Souq Waqif سوق واقف -: *Opening Hours* - 06:00-14:00 / 15:00-20:00 Sat-Fri -: *Phone* - +974 7745 1196 -: *Email* - info@inboundtoursqatar.com -: *WebSite* - www.inboundtoursqatar.com -: *Description* - Tours throughout Qatar, including Desert Safari, with optional overnight, and Dhow trips.

QATAR INTERNATIONAL ADVENTURES -: *GPS* 25.270208, 51.517262 -: *Street* - 1st Floor, Office # 7, 16 Al Rawabi St -: *Public Transport if available* - Bus 21,22,94 -: *Area* - Rawdat Al Khail روضة الخيل -: *Opening Hours* - 08:30-21:00 Sat-Thurs 08:30-17:00 Fri -: *Phone* - +974 4455 3954 -: *Email* - info@qia-qatar.com -: *WebSite* - www.qia-qatar.com -: *Description* - City tours, Desert Safari, Dhow Cruise, Game Fishing, Helicopter,

Q-EXPLORER -: *GPS* 25.317781, 51.528357 -: *Street* - Doha Tower, Al Corniche -: *Public Transport if available* - Bus 76,777 Metro Red Line WestBay -: *Area* - West Bay الخليج الغربي -: *Phone* - +974 4472 5146 -: *Email* - info@q-explorer.com -: *WebSite* - www.q-explorer.com -: *Description* - City Tours, Desert Safari, Kayaking, Scuba,

REGATTA SAILING ACADEMY -: *GPS* 25.353970, 51.528703 -: *Street* - off Lusail Expressway (south Katara) -: *Public Transport if available* - Metro Red Line Al Qassar -: *Area* - Katara كتارا -: *Opening Hours* - 09:00-17:00 -: *Phone* - +974 5550 3484 -: *Email* - simon@regattasailingacademy.com -: *WebSite* - www.regat-tasailingacademy.com -: *Description* - Sailboat and training for other craft.

SKYDIVE QATAR -: *GPS* 25.701115, 51.361709 -: *Street* - Al Shamal Rd -: *Public Transport if available* - no public transport -: *Area* - Al Khor (13kilometres west of town - final 2 kilometres are on well graded but rough track الخور) -: *Opening Hours* - 07:00-17:00 Mon-Sat -: *Cost* QAR1150(upwards) -: *Phone* - +974 40329173 -: *Email* - info@skydiveqatar.com -: *WebSite* - www.skydiveqatar.com -: *Description* - Plunge from a plane over central Qatar - with views of course of land, sea and lots of sky. Booking essential.

CHAPTER THIRTY

INDEX

CPSIA information can be obtained
at www.ICGtesting.com
Printed in the USA
BVHW051515040320
574094BV00002B/12

9 781999 813581